Projections

Projections

Our World of
Imaginary Relationships

James Halpern, PhD
Ilsa Halpern

Seaview/Putnam
NEW YORK

The authors gratefully acknowledge permission from the following sources to
quote material in the text:

Princeton University Press for material from *The Collected Works of C. G.
Jung* by C. G. Jung, translated by R. F. C. Hall, Bollingen Series XX, Vol.
1-15. Copyright © 1953-1973 by Princeton University Press.

W. W. Norton & Company, Inc., for material from *Civilization and Its Discontents* by Sigmund Freud, edited and translated by James Strachey. Copyright © 1961 by James Strachey.

Alfred A. Knopf, Inc., for material from *Something Happened* by Joseph
Heller. Copyright © 1966 by Scapegoat Productions, Inc.

Library of Congress Cataloging in Publication Data

Halpern, James.
    Projections: our world of imaginary relationships.

    1. Projection (Psychology) 2. Interpersonal relations.
3. Psychology, Pathological. I. Halpern, Ilsa.
II. Title.
BF175.H34   1983   150.19′5   82-19230
ISBN 0-399-31017-7

Printed in the United States of America

Acknowledgments

We would first like to thank all the people who took the time to fill out the questionnaires and be interviewed. Thanks also to our capable research assistants Piri Brandt, Lori Freedman, Rose Mastrovito, and Linda Ross, who helped develop, distribute, and analyze the questionnaires we used. The information provided by Denny Albee, Cynthia Bostick, Lynne Dorsey, Lisa May, Susan Mende, Stephen Schaefer, James Seymour, Shelley Sherman, Linda Watson, and Congressman Theodore Weiss was especially appreciated.

Joyce Frommer and Diana Price provided many suggestions and were instrumental in launching the project. Cameron Barry's careful reading and advice helped us in a number of chapters. We benefited greatly from the hard work of two editors. Anne Kostick did a superb job editing the manuscript. She helped us shape the book and made insightful comments and useful suggestions from beginning to end. Christine Schillig did the final editing and transformed the manuscript into a book. The conscientious work of our typists Susan Davison, Lisa Monti, and Christine Ross, made our work much easier.

Finally, we would like to thank our parents, Tuz and Curley Mende and Myrna and Henry Seigle, for their love and support.

For Nathan Benjamin

Contents

Projections

1

What Is Projection?

Elizabeth is an attractive woman with blue eyes and red, curly hair. She did her undergraduate work at a small, prestigious New England college and recently received her master's degree in business administration. When she went job hunting, she was able to choose from three good jobs. Elizabeth selected a growing communications company, where she is earning an excellent starting salary. At age twenty-eight, she began intensive psychotherapy. The reason she began therapy was that she was extremely unhappy with her work—a common "presenting problem." Although periodically Elizabeth's work was boring, her primary difficulty was with the people around her. "I don't feel comfortable with anyone. Some of the people I work with are shallow and insincere. It makes me feel awful to be around them, and I have a terrible problem with my administrative assistant. She's sloppy and doesn't care at all about her work. Almost every time I look over a report she's done for me, I'm furious and close to tears because of my assistant's incompetence."

Since adolescence, Elizabeth almost always had a boyfriend, yet no relationship gave her what she wanted—intimacy and marriage. Recently she fell in love with a man named Elliot, ten years older than she, who seemed to love her as much as she did him. They had a marvelous romance, seeing each other every day, going to the beach, on picnics, to concerts, and spending a lot of time in bed. But Elliot, who had not long before separated from his wife and two daughters, decided to go back to his family. Elizabeth, who had been so elated by the affair, was deeply depressed.

It became clear in the course of therapy that many of the problems Elizabeth had were not caused by people or circumstances but by her projections. The process of psychological projection is very much like the mechanical process of projecting a movie upon a screen. The "film" is our own private home movies, our own conscious and unconscious characteristics, desires, experiences. The "screen" is the other person. Instead of seeing someone else clearly, we unknowingly project our own images upon them. So what we're seeing is part of ourselves. It's easy to see how this can lead to incredible misunderstanding and conflict. While we think we are engaged in a dialogue with another person, we are in fact, to some degree, in a monologue with ourselves. We are in a hall of mirrors. We are seeing a mirage, an image made from our own psyche. This, then, is our definition of *projection: the blurred perception of another person that arises because we are seeing an aspect of ourselves rather than the other.*

Like Elizabeth, everyone sees and often must deal with people who have unpleasant, aggravating qualities. But why are we so deeply disturbed by some and not by others? And how is it that some people do not come undone when they see problems or weaknesses in others? The answer lies in the fact that we are most affected—irritated or fascinated—by people who exhibit those very qualities we too possess, whether or not we are aware of it.

We would expect Elizabeth to be concerned about an administrative assistant who doesn't care about her job, but because Elizabeth is unaware of her own desires to be irresponsible, because she unconsciously resents doing her own work, she is especially upset. When we refuse to acknowledge our own feelings, we see them, often in exaggerated form, in someone else—and feel outraged and undone.

Clearly, not all our problems are due to projection. Elizabeth's difficulties involve other people. These are the kinds of problems psychotherapists are best equipped to deal with. Psychotherapy cannot be of much help to people who are troubled because they don't have enough money to fix their car or send their children to expensive schools, nor can it be especially effective with people who are poor because they lack the skills necessary to get a good job. Such problems and many like them have little to do with psychotherapy or projection. But most of the problems that therapists treat involve other people. What we can understand and accept in ourselves we have no need to project. We can therefore admire or dislike a quality in someone else but see it without projection.

Most of psychotherapy involves educating, encouraging, analyzing, and sometimes forcing a client to understand and let go of projections. The therapist usually challenges the client's views of himself and others and suggests alternate ways to perceive the same situation. This is the process of identifying and letting go of projection and it happens in most therapeutic situations no matter what the therapist's orientation happens to be.

Projections are not confined to the therapist's office. They arise because the way we see those around us depends on who we are. Our needs, many of them unconscious, obscure those around us. Recent experiments done by J. Halpern and others with normal adults have verified that projection is part of our daily lives and is not an indication of abnormal or disturbed functioning.[1]

In the sixth game of the 1980 World Series, Pete Rose of the Philadelphia Phillies came sliding home with what would have been the tying run. The umpire called him out, to the thunderous disapproval of sixty thousand fans in Veterans Stadium and millions more watching at home. They didn't want a favor from the umpire; their eyes told them that Rose was safe. The Kansas City fans didn't see it that way at all. Gather five eyewitnesses to a crime together. Ask them to describe the assailant, the victim, the sequence of events. More often than not, you will get five different versions—often dramatically different versions—of the "same" event.

The way we see the world around us has a great deal to do with who *we* are and what *we* want and need. Just as, to a hungry man, a rock on the ground might momentarily look like a piece of fruit, for all of us, our desires change the way things appear. It's not too hard to accept the fact that our perception of objects is often quite subjective. Sunbathers lying on a beach describing the lazy drift of clouds above them often see very different things. But what about the way in which we see other people, what we think and feel about them? Can it be that we don't really know and understand those around us, that the way we see them is as subjective as the way we see clouds? The answer to both these questions is yes—and a discussion of why this is so is what this book is about.

"Just as we tend to assume that the world is as we see it," said C. G. Jung, "we naively suppose that people are as we imagine them to be. In this way everyone creates a series of imaginary relationships based essentially on projection."[2] It may be hard for us to accept what Jung was telling us. However, years of research and clinical practice have convinced us that he was right. Projection is an extremely potent force in people's lives. Because of it, the link between them and other people is not a direct one.

We project our own needs, experiences, and feelings. These get in the way, obscuring our vision and confusing our understanding.

Centuries ago, the material world was mysterious, and people projected aspects of themselves onto the physical objects around them. They saw gods, princes, and princesses in clouds; they saw winged horses, bulls, archers in the stars; demons in caves; wisdom in trees.

It has been a slow and painful process, but science has gradually forced us to remove our projections from the physical world. Materials no longer seem so mysterious or so fascinating as they did centuries ago. Today we do not worship the sun or become excited by the moon. By withdrawing our projections, we have established a more objective relationship to these objects. Once in a while on a dark night in the woods or on a city street, our projections cause the world to come alive again with spirits and demons, but it is much more likely that other people and not objects will be the targets for our projections.

We may know and understand the physical world, but we do not at all understand ourselves and each other. Why do we wake up one morning feeling vaguely uneasy or depressed and fine the next day? Why do we find someone boring one day and interesting the next? Why do we repeat our same mistakes, overlook things we shouldn't, feel irritable for no apparent reason? Most of us have virtually no idea why we do as we do, feel as we feel, or think what we think. Our lack of self-understanding is only matched by our lack of understanding of others. This is because what we don't understand in ourselves, we project. This leads to relationships based on projection, which is an unconscious connection.

Projection is the kind of idea that makes many people uncomfortable; it is a difficult notion to swallow. All of us count on the accuracy of our perceptions; we like to believe that we see others clearly, that we really know the people around us. However, our world of relationships is largely of our own construction. Because of projection, we inevitably face disappointment and confusion. But it is possible for us to understand and overcome our projections, enabling us to have more satisfying relationships and happier lives. Out of the confusion of fantasy can emerge the real people in our lives—our parents, our children, our friends, our co-workers, our lovers.

Many of us feel that fostering our own growth must be separate from nurturing and maintaining the growth of our relationships—whatever the relationship might be. There is a popular notion that this is an either/or proposition, that is, we can either become complete people on our own or else sacrifice our own independence for the sake of maintaining healthy relationships. So, many people have abandoned relationships in the interest of self-growth. Because they blame those around them for their difficulties, they think that by leaving, they are taking a brave and constructive step. Americans have been blaming and leaving parents, blaming and leaving spouses and children, blaming and leaving bosses and co-workers and friends at ever-increasing rates.

This response to problems is a legacy from the seventies. Although that decade is over, many people still follow the philosophy that when things get to be too much, the best thing to do is leave. However, solving our difficulties this way usually doesn't work. This is because we take ourselves and our projections wherever we go.

Therefore, the cause of our problems with other people doesn't leave the moment we quit the scene. Projections demand to be dealt with or else they will continue to haunt us, following in every subsequent marriage, friendship, and job situation. We must become aware of them.

Projection is an especially useful concept for tackling our interpersonal problems precisely because it deals at one and the same time with personal and interpersonal growth; the two are intertwined. As we begin to unravel the intricacies of projections in our dealings with those around us, we are at the same time gaining an understanding of ourselves. This is because what we project comes from within us—from our conscious and unconscious selves. By getting to know the form and content of our projections, we learn about our own psychological makeup.

Elizabeth began therapy because while others thought her life was going well, she didn't. Getting up and going to work in the morning took a lot out of her. She began to come to work late, often by fifteen minutes, sometimes by half an hour. She was beginning to feel that people in the office were talking about her—especially about her lateness. Elizabeth was also preoccupied with thoughts of Elliot. Although their affair had been brief, she was sure that he would have been a perfect partner. He was charming, witty, strong yet sensitive. Also there was the matter of her car accidents. Whenever things began to go well for Elizabeth, she would have one. There had been four such incidents in the past three years, and after each one, she would feel depressed for weeks. Estimates had to be gotten, reports filled out, repairs had to be negotiated—and life without a car was just plain difficult. Elizabeth experienced her life as a knot of confusion. She was very unclear about where one problem ended and another began. Her psychotherapy involved untangling these knots, which were made of her projections. Each relationship had to be examined in order to discover which projections were operating, so she could see and distinguish herself from the other person. There are several types of projection, and different ones operate in different circumstances. These will be discussed in Chapter 2. That chapter also contains a discussion of how psychologists and psychiatrists have recognized the part played by projection in the development of psychopathology since Freud introduced the term in the late 1800s.

The projection process begins before we are born. As Elizabeth was growing up, many things were projected onto her by her parents—but none was more troublesome than her parent's unexpressed, often unconscious conflicts. They were frequently unable to resolve their differences with each other and projected their doubts, misgivings, and resentments about each other onto Elizabeth. She became what was projected onto her—a problem child. Elizabeth's present car accidents perpetuate this projection. She is tied to her parents by them. After each accident, she calls her father, who has contacts with garages and insurance companies. Her parents commiserate about their problem child, and the pattern continues. Projection in parent-child relationships is discussed in Chapter 3.

Elizabeth's unresolved conflicts with her parents are carried over into her couple relationships (Chapter 4). Her problems with men are caused by her projection of parental images onto them that they cannot or will not fulfill. Her boyfriends at some point in the relationship disappoint her because they do not play the part of the father who would entertain, take care of, make decisions for, cheer up daddy's little girl. Her frequent infatuations arise when she sees the undeveloped masculine side of herself in a man, falls in love with it, and is then disappointed when he cannot be this image. Her ensuing difficulties with men are caused by the clash between the mythic projection of an ideal dream boy and the reality of the other person (Loss of Love, Chapter 5).

On the job (Chapter 6), many of Elizabeth's projections are clearly seen. Here is where she spends most of her time and psychological energy. Elizabeth's mild paranoia about her fellow workers was explained by Freud some eighty years ago. She is unable to recognize her own asocial feelings, her own desires to shirk responsibility, so she pins them on her assistant. Her feelings of self-reproach or self-criticism are also unconscious, and these are projected onto co-workers. Rather than criticize herself, she feels reproached by them—they are thinking about her, talking about her. This causes her paranoia.

Psychotherapists attempt to uncover their patients' unconscious conflicts, using a wide variety of techniques such as the analysis of dreams, slips of the tongue and pen, and transference (the patient's feelings about the analyst). But our unconscious conflicts—the disowned, disassociated aspects of ourselves—are apparent in what we see and are bothered by in the people around us.

Elizabeth's therapy was effective because over a period of months she was able to recognize her various projections and thereby understand herself and others better. Research shows that clients like Elizabeth—intelligent, motivated, articulate— are most likely to make the most effective use of psychotherapy.[3] These are the qualities that are essential to recognizing and dissolving projections. What is also needed is a willingness to consider that we live in a flimsy world of imaginary relationships and a desire to make them real.

We offer one example to illustrate how Elizabeth dissolved her projections. In order to see her administrative assistant more clearly, she had to recognize her own negative feelings about the job. She had to develop insight into her desire to shirk responsibility. Then she had to integrate these negative feelings into the many positive ones she had about her job. When she was able to do this, the result was a more complex or differentiated and ambivalent attitude toward her work and also a more complex and accepting view of her assistant. In the process of incorporating her projections, she no longer had to project her self-criticisms onto her co-workers, and her paranoia was reduced. The other benefit that comes from dissolving projections is that the psychological energy invested in inner conflict and irritation with other people is taken back and reinvested in activities with greater return. She thus had more energy to wake up and get to work on time, and much more enthusiasm for her work.

Historian Daniel Boorstin, now librarian of Congress, warned some twenty years ago that Americans are threatened by a new and peculiar menace: the menace of unreality. "We risk being the first people in history to have been able to make their illusions so vivid, so persuasive, so realistic that they can live in them. We are the most illusioned people on earth. Yet we dare not become disillusioned, because our illusions are the very house in which we live; they are our news, our heros, our adventure, our forms of art, our very existence."[4]

In chapters 7 and 8, there is a discussion of how many individuals find one target upon whom they can project mythic images. Some of our most intense illusions exist in the connection between ourselves and celebrities in the worlds of entertainment and sport. Although in most cases, we have never and will never meet or know these stars, they are nonetheless a real part of our lives. Think for a moment of a favorite entertainer or athlete. Often we feel we know these people quite well. If asked, we could probably give elaborate descriptions of their personalities. Some people go far beyond admiration and become passionate about them. We are all familiar with symptoms of this fan fever, but what are its causes? Where do these feelings and thoughts come from, and what makes us feel so strongly about these strangers? Their presence, their carefully sculpted images trigger in us a depth and variety of emotions that go far beyond the entertainers themselves. We react to our unknown faces, or projections. The stars are the targets for our dream boy, dream girl, and hero projections.

Boorstin suggests that Americans value their illusions, and this is true—but only to some extent. Within each of us, there is a strong desire to break down the illusions in order to see the people around us clearly. We are fascinated by our projections, but at the same time, we are cynical people. And cynicism is an important first step in the recognition of our projections. We come to doubt or be suspicious of our reactions to others. We wonder if a politician will really perform as miraculously as he promises and we think. We are skeptical of people who tell us that their children are princes or their parents are saints or their lovers are perfect and magical. However, although cynicism is an important step in the process of dissolving projection, it is not the final one. When cynicism causes disappointment, we often just hang our projections on new hooks. This process itself may be helpful if disappointment eventually leads us to discover that what we have been seeing and seeking in others are aspects of our own personalities.

It is very hard work to dissolve our projections. To do so means to take responsibility for our lives. It is much easier to give all the blame and credit for our emotions to the people around us. But when parts of ourselves are given to others through projection, we are correspondingly less than what we are capable of being. Our undeveloped potential is trapped in our projections.

Projections are very common and also very "real." They are real because although they are phantoms or visions, they have pronounced effects. The medieval epidemics of bubonic plague did not cause as many deaths as did the desperate projection of the savior image by millions onto a former corporal in Nazi Germany. Understanding and overcoming our projections is not an idle or self-indulgent task. In a very real sense, it is only by taking back and dissolving our projections that we can come in contact with the real world.

It is not easy to differentiate between an objective relationship and one based on projection. Almost always our relationships combine both. Sorting out our illusions from reality is work that takes a lifetime. Throughout the book, the clues that signal the working of projection will be pointed out, but there are no foolproof answers.

In the final analysis, it makes sense to look at our thoughts and feelings about other people as projections if by doing so we get to know ourselves and them a little better. The approach taken in this book is thus purely pragmatic. If you and your partner are not getting along, see what happens if you attempt to dissolve and become your projections. If you are fighting with your parents or children or friends, you may try to take back or identify with those qualities you attribute to them. If you find a hero at work or in the community who fascinates you, see what happens if you share in those qualities. If understanding and owning your projections helps you be more effective and competent in the world and have more satisfying relationships, then the concepts and ideas presented here are real because they are useful for you.

2
Historical Roots

Psychologists get their ideas for research from many different sources. Not the least of these is our personal experience, which plays a large role in determining what we study.

Although the initial motivation for this book was personal experience, we relied on many other sources for gathering our information: news events, literary writings, questionnaires, interviews, and experimental studies. We have also relied on the ideas and work of other psychologists. Scientific research is a cumulative process in which scientists build upon the theories and research of the past. Most psychologists recognize this and, before presenting their own contributions, cite previous research, giving credit where it is due. We want to do this now.

Projective Tests

Since Sigmund Freud first used the term in a letter to Fliess in 1895,[1] the concept of projection has continued to be of use and interest to psychologists. It has been studied in clinics and consulting rooms as well as in the laboratory. When psychologists evaluate and study people's personalities, they have two major types of tests at their disposal: objective and projective. With an objective test, an evaluater tries to measure traits and characteristics according to how the person answers a series of straightforward questions. For example, someone who agrees with the statement, "I frequently lose my temper and shout a lot around the house," would be seen as more hostile than someone who does not.

But people may not be able or willing to reveal their attitudes and feelings directly, and this is when projective tests can be most valuable. The psychologist may present a series of drawings of people in various situations and ask, "What is happening in this picture? What are these people doing, what are they thinking, and what will happen?" If a person examines a picture of someone looking out the window and says, "He is probably thinking whether or not to jump," and such themes and stories continue to be seen in other pictures, the psychologist may conclude that the person is depressed. Psychologists believe that people project inner concerns onto all sorts of ambiguous stimuli. They have constructed special tests, using pictures (TAT tests), inkblots (Rorschach tests), and unfinished sentences (sentence-completion tests), in order to prompt or encourage people to project and reveal aspects of themselves that would otherwise be difficult to discover. For example, one TAT card shows a boy sitting down at the table with a violin in front of him. One patient looks at the card and says the boy is thinking about becoming a great musician someday. Another looks at the card and says that the boy has been forced to practice and is trying to figure out how to get away from his parents. It is clear that both are projecting their own conflicts, attitudes, and concerns.

If you listen to five people discussing their reactions to a movie, a restaurant, or a painting, you can often discover more about the people than about the objects they are describing. Our needs, concerns and personalities cannot be excluded from our perceptions and reactions.

The biggest problem in using projective tests as diagnostic instruments is that psychologists seldom agree on how to interpret them. If you look at an inkblot and say, "I see two large mountains," one psychologist might say you are projecting a need to overcome great obstacles while another might say you are projecting an unresolved sexual feeling for your mother. Although projective tests are imprecise, most psychologists do believe that in the hands of a skilled clinician, they can provide rich, interesting, and valuable information.

Definitions

Many definitions of projection have been offered, but most have been criticized for being too broad and inclusive. One suggestion was "the manifestation of behavior by an individual which indicates some emotional need of the individual."[2] If this broad definition of projection were accepted, eating, sleeping, and sex might all have to be considered projections, since they could indicate our emotional needs. Henry Murray, who developed the TAT and researched projection, said, "If projection means everything it means nothing."[3]

In order to keep projection from meaning too much, some psychologists have tried to break the term down into manageable parts. By developing a classification system, it is hoped that the term will not be too unwieldy, too vague, or too broad.

Our definition—the blurred perception of another caused by attributing one's own traits to the other—is amplified in this book by a new classification system. We propose three types or levels of projection.

The first level is *parallel projection,** which is the tendency to see others as we see ourselves. We simply attribute aspects of ourselves that we are aware of onto others. It is the most superficial level of projection, the easiest to investigate experimentally, and the one for which there is the most experimental evidence.

The second level, *unconscious projection,* corresponds to Freud's ideas about projection. He felt that one of the ways we defend ourselves against our own painful or unacceptable feelings or impulses is to be unaware of them in ourselves—to repress them—and then to see them in other people. This sort of projection, as a defense mechanism, is used and discussed by Freud and his followers, but there is less experimental research to support it than there is for parallel projection. It is very difficult to investigate scientifically ideas or feelings that are said to be unconscious.

There is much clinical but little experimental evidence for our third level of projection—*mythic projection*—which is based on Carl Jung's theory of psychology and psychotherapy. Jung believed that everyone, throughout the ages and in all places, is fascinated by the same types of images or ideas. He called these images *archetypes,* and he found evidence for them in legends, folk tales, myths, religion, and fairy tales throughout history and from all over the world. Jung suggested that when we are unaware of these powerful archetypal images in ourselves, we have a tendency to project them outward.

We'll turn now to a discussion of the research and theory that pertain to each of the three levels of projection.

---

*In the experimental literature, this process is most often referred to as attributive projection.

Parallel Projections

The first experimental study of parallel projection was done in 1942, when Beatrice Wright asked children to pick their favorite toy from a group of toys and to choose one to give to another child.[4] She then asked the child to suppose that another child was given the same choice. "Which toy would the other child give away?" Generous children—those who gave up a favorite toy— guessed that other children would be similarly generous, while children who held on to their favorite figured that another child would not give up his or her favorite, either. Some years later, Elizabeth Mintz asked children from five to fourteen to watch a cartoon film of Peter Pan and then guess his age.[5] The five-year-olds guessed he was five, the six-year-olds said he was six, the nine-year-olds nine, and so forth.

Children use parallel projections. But what about adults; do they too use parallel projections? Research studies show that happy college students see other college students as happy, whereas unhappy college students tend to see others as unhappy.[6] In another study, adults were asked to predict the inner thoughts and feelings of other people. Their predictions turned out to be remarkably parallel to their own.[7]

Currently there are two models that account for why we see other people as being like ourselves. Neither has been completely confirmed. The first approach was suggested by one of Freud's best-known students and critics, Karen Horney. She said that parallel projections are due to naiveté. We foolishly assume that other people "feel or react in the same manner that we ourselves do."[8] If Horney is right, it would seem that as people got older or smarter, or both, they would be less likely to use parallel projections.

Maybe it takes intelligence to realize that just because you like the Yankees, turtleneck shirts, and hot chocolate, not everyone does. J. Halpern and a colleague, Anne Myers, did two experiments to see if there was any clear connection between age or intellectual development and the use of parallel projection.[9] There wasn't. Maybe *emotional*, not intellectual, maturity is the crucial factor in determining parallel projection. That is, perhaps more emotionally mature individuals would not be as likely to use parallel projections. As yet, there is no research that tests this possibility.

Another way of trying to understand parallel projection involves the idea of defense. Although we don't like to admit it, most of us have a good deal of insecurity. When we come into contact with other people, we often experience nervousness and tension. We wonder if we will be liked or accepted. Will we be ignored, not respected, or perhaps even denigrated?

Our fears are not entirely groundless. As Freud once said, most of our greatest hurts have come not from nature or physical pain but from other people. One way we can make other people less threatening—one way to defend ourselves—is to see them as being similar to us. We hope that someone who looks and sounds as we do will be more friendly. We suspect (and there is much evidence to support this view) that people who share our attitudes and values will be more agreeable.

When we meet people, we often reveal through our conversation or body language very small bits of ourselves ("nice weather we're having") and look to see if there are signs of agreement (friendliness) or similarity before proceeding to more intimate forms of communication. Even talking about the weather is not entirely safe. People have been known to respond, "Blah! I can't stand sunny days. They are so boring. I much prefer extreme cold or sticky humidity." At this point, one is not likely to begin a discussion of love or religion.

Rather than wait to see if someone really "resembles" us, we simply see ourselves in other people. We use parallel projection to make the world more secure and less threatening. We are most likely to do this when we have feelings or ideas we are not comfortable about. If we cheat on exams or on our taxes, we feel better believing that others are doing the same. In these instances, we are threatened by our own feelings, thoughts, or actions, and so we defend ourselves by using parallel projections. "If everyone cheats, then I'm not really cheating very much, and maybe cheating isn't so bad." If you use parallel projection to defend yourself against your own questionable attributes, whom are you likely to project upon? An awful, disliked, or very dissimilar person is not a good target. It won't make you feel better to think, "I cheat on taxes, but so did Al Capone and other convicted felons." Not much comfort there. It may, however, make you feel better to project onto other reasonable, honest people. As long as you see other decent, honest people cheating, you feel better about the fact that you do. Many people do in fact cheat on their income taxes, but people who cheat probably overestimate the percentage of others who do so.

Someone we interviewed described his sadomasochistic sexual practices. He described how pain was an essential part of sexuality. When we mentioned that this need not be so, he quickly said, "Look, there are millions of people who are into the same stuff that I am, and those who are not doing it want to." This is a clear case of parallel projection. We asked what kinds of people are involved in these sadomasochistic practices. As you might guess, an answer that serves self-defensive functions would not be "weirdos, cranks, and other perverts." In fact, his answer was "business people, professionals, and lots of entertainers." The proper target for a parallel projection is a liked other.

One other variable involved with this type of projection is the self-image of the person who is projecting. It seems ironic, but the person with the most self-esteem is most likely to use parallel projection as a defense.[10] This is because a person with little self-esteem or a poor self-image has nothing to defend. If you think you are a worthless person and you cheat on your taxes, why should you need to think other people cheat on their taxes? Cheating goes hand in hand with the fact that you know you are not good. But if you think highly of yourself—if you have high self-esteem—then you have something to protect and you may distort other people in order to keep your own bad qualities from looking too bad. Quite probably there is both an element of defensiveness and an element of naiveté behind parallel projections.

Whether or not we are aware of possessing the quality we project greatly affects the target for the projections. If you are aware of having homosexual tendencies, you will tend to see other liked or admired people as having them. But if you have them and are not aware of it, you may see these qualities in disliked and dissimilar others. Of course, the person who was responsible for calling our attention to the possibility that we may have all sorts of unpleasant feelings, ideas, and impulses that we are unaware of was Freud. We have never looked the same to ourselves since.

Unconscious Projection

Many psychologists believe that Freud's most important contribution was his work on the psychological defense mechanisms. Freud discovered that we have many socially and personally unacceptable feelings and thoughts which are very painful. We therefore force them out of our consciousness or never allow them to enter our awareness in the first place. This is the process of psychological *repression*, and it is, in Freud's own words, the cornerstone of his entire theory. When we repress, we are protecting ourselves from ourselves. We try to preserve a good self-image and to reduce anxiety. However, if we overuse this self-protection, we pay a price. In fact, we may wind up sick or neurotic because so much psychic energy is used to keep ourselves ignorant of our own feelings. Although almost all Freud's work has been criticized, much of it still stands as useful and important, and none of it more so than his ideas about defenses.

For Freud, projection was a mechanism of defense. To repress an impulse like sex or aggression serves a defensive function, but to see this impulse in someone else, to focus on the other person instead of on ourselves, helps to reinforce this defense. If repression is the most important way we can defend ourselves, projection is a second line of defense. Being overly concerned with other people's negative traits helps us remain unaware of our own.

In the next few pages, we attempt to show how Freud used projection to explain several forms of psychopathology and the transference relationship.

Paranoia

Very early in his career, Freud recognized the importance of projection. In a letter to Fliess in 1895,[11] he examined the causes of paranoia. Why do some people feel persecuted when there are no persecutors? Why do some people feel mistrustful and suspicious when there are no grounds for it? The cause, of course, is within. If we are aware of or in touch with all our various thoughts and feelings, there would be much for us to criticize, but we are not so aware, and we spare ourselves thereby this self-criticism. We think of ourselves as decent, understanding, and self-respecting, and there is little for which we condemn ourselves. But other people, damn them, are thinking bad thoughts about us. They are critical and condemning, and we are distrustful and sensitive to them.

According to Freud, the paranoid always pleads his own innocence. He refuses to criticize or condemn himself. Instead of reproaching himself for some unacceptable thought or feeling, he projects the reproach or condemnations. It may be easier for the paranoid to cope with the imagined criticism or reproaches from others than to face his own self-criticism and ponder its true causes.

According to Freud, if we look carefully within ourselves, we will find much to frighten and terrify us. On the conscious level, we may love and respect a parent or compete with a sibling; on the unconscious level, we may have impulses to sleep with the parent or kill the sibling. Freud didn't think people were only killers and rapists, but he believed we had some of these feelings. He was also convinced that we were better off knowing about them than remaining unaware. One of the consequences of not knowing about an internal threat—a frightening feeling from within—is that we might see the source of our fear as outside (projection) rather than coming from the inside. The paranoid projects an internal threat, and instead of fearing himself becomes terrified of other people.

Phobias

It is also possible to project one's dangerous feelings not onto people but onto physical objects or animals.[12] Actually this seems to be a more adaptive pathology than paranoia. It is possible to defend oneself from unconscious fears by projecting them onto closed or open spaces or water or high places. Phobias are irrational fears, and almost no one is without a few. They are discovered and named quite frequently. One recent addition is *arachibutyrophobia,* which is the fear of peanut butter sticking to the roof of your mouth. Take a group of people to the top of a tall building or through a tunnel or into the reptile house at the zoo and you will find significant numbers of them feeling uncomfortable and even getting ill. Our own dangerous impulses, without our awareness, are projected outward and distort the world around us, giving it a morbid quality.

If phobias are kept within bounds, a feared object can be a convenient target for repressed and projected wishes. If you have a fear of snakes, for instance, you can just stay away from zoos, tall grass, and people who have them as pets. Your life is not likely to suffer greatly, and you are simultaneously protecting yourself from the knowledge that you possess some unacceptable feelings. However, if you are frightened of elevators, cars, offices, and all animals to the extent that you cannot leave your home, the phobia is much less adaptive and more problematic. Freud would treat such a condition by helping the patient gradually gain insight into what the internal fear is. The goal is to eliminate the need to project. Both paranoia and phobias develop when we are unable to face ourselves and instead find an external fear by way of projection.

Insight

The goal of Freudian psychotherapy or psychoanalysis is insight. The impulses that are outside of our awareness do not cease to exist. They push and pull us around so we don't really know what we are doing. We form and break relationships, take up and leave jobs, and make many other important decisions without all the necessary information. For example, someone may get into one destructive relationship after another while never understanding how he could do such things. He feels that things continually work out badly; he is always victimized, always unlucky. Psychoanalysis may uncover a repressed desire to hurt a parent—a parent who may have hoped more than anything for this person to be in a good relationship. The destructive relationships cause the parent pain, and that is what the person really wants to accomplish—unconsciously. Now that he knows about this wish and it is no longer unconscious, he may yell at the parent or hurt him in some other way, but he no longer needs to get into awful relationships in order to satisfy the unconscious wish.

Insight gives the client more information, more choices, freedom. It also means a more complicated and differentiated sense of self. It means recognizing that we are not perfect. It may not be easy to acknowledge angry feelings toward a parent. However, the recognition of these feelings may bring about the breakdown of projection. Psychoanalysis attempts to replace neurosis with normal human suffering. The course this process takes is clear in Freud's discussion of delusional jealousy.

Delusional Jealousy

Freud treated several patients who were so consumed by jealousy that they were unable to function in the world. There are men and women who are so convinced that their partners are unfaithful that they tap their own phone or pretend to go to work and hide in the bushes, waiting for the expected lover. They are afraid to go to public places or to social gatherings with their spouse for fear a new liaison will be made. If the partner buys a new shirt or takes a shower or goes out to buy a paper, it is seen as a sign of infidelity. Every action, every movement, and every gesture is transformed into a threatening one by someone who is jealous. Sometimes, of course, such suspicions are justified. However, in many cases, they are completely out of touch with the reality of the situation. This is when jealousy is called delusional.

What is the cause of such extreme and unrealistic mistrust? The condition seems to resemble paranoia, with its suspiciousness and exaggerated fears. Freud's explanation should be apparent. He pointed out that even though people get married, they may still feel sexually attracted to others. This may not be startling news today, but when Freud wrote his paper in 1922,[13] there were people who did not agree with his suggestion that the kind of fidelity that is required in marriage is maintained in the face of constant temptation. Delusional jealousy comes about when someone refuses to believe that he or she has impulses toward faithlessness, denies and represses such feelings, and projects them onto the partner. "Our jealous husband perceived his wife's unfaithfulness instead of his own," said Freud. "By becoming conscious of hers and magnifying enormously he succeeded in keeping his own unconscious."[14]

Someone crazed with jealousy misperceives, exaggerates, and distorts a partner due to projection. This can only come about when a person refuses to recognize or come to terms with his or her own feelings of being sexually attracted to other people. Such feelings—impulses toward infidelity—can be quite threatening and potentially disruptive. The fear that they could lead to infidelity and possibly destroy the primary relationship leads some people to bury them. The repressed feelings do not disappear but return with added force in the form of projection. Since it is more than likely that everyone has such impulses, a person suffering from delusional jealousy is rarely considered mad for suspecting the partner of infidelity. The partner probably does have such impulses. The partner is then a suitable hook upon which the projection is hung. By focusing, concentrating, and paying so much attention to the partner's feelings, the delusionally jealous person is distracted and protected from being aware of his or her own feelings.

Transference

One of Freud's most important and useful discoveries was that projection plays a major role in the relationship between psychotherapist and patient. Early in his career, while he was using hypnosis as a therapeutic technique, a female patient awoke from a trance and threw her arms around him. He knew that her reaction was not due to his own irresistibility, and he was determined to discover the source of this intense reaction.

It was this incident that convinced Freud to stop using hypnosis altogether. He wanted to try to understand his patients' feelings about him. This was difficult to accomplish with the patient in a trance. He continued to find that from the moment therapy began, his patients would react very strongly to him. Some would fall in love almost immediately; they thought he was all-knowing. Others would just as suddenly develop an intense hatred. As you can imagine, Freud found this very disturbing. One patient would be trying to seduce him, another talking about killing him. Freud realized that these reactions were not caused by his personality. He called this phenomenon *the transference;* his patients were not seeing and reacting to him but to something else. Freud's interpretation was that many of the patient's unresolved, unexpressed childhood emotions were brought into the therapeutic situation and transferred onto the therapist. Such a transfer totally distorts the way the therapist is perceived. Freud wrote in 1910 that the transference is actually a specific form of projection.[15]

Because of this discovery, Freud strongly urged psychotherapists not to get emotionally involved with their clients. If a client yells at a therapist, it is inappropriate for the therapist to yell back. If a client wants to sleep with a therapist, a therapist should not consent. Freud believed that the therapist's job is to help the patient understand himself better, not to become a friend, an enemy, or a lover. The patient can find such relationships outside of therapy.

The feelings that a client has for a therapist should therefore not be indulged, but neither should they be ignored. The analyst remains detached—emotionally uninvolved—and in this way presents a blank screen for the patient to project upon. The patient's feelings about the analyst can then be interpreted and analyzed and understood as part of the patient's psychology. In one of Freud's earliest cases, he treated a woman named Dora, who had strong feelings for her father and transferred these feelings onto Freud. Dora ran away from therapy just as she had run away from her father.[16] At the time, Freud did not fully understand the power of the transference, but later he saw that past actions, conflicts, and problems are almost invariably presented in the therapy itself. The therapist's job is to show the patient that many current feelings are projections, based on past experience, which must be dissolved and understood.

For Freud and all those who follow him, recognizing, dealing with, and working through the transference is the most important part of the therapeutic work. "This struggle between the doctor and the patient," Freud wrote, "between intellectual and instinctual life, between understanding and seeking to act, is played out almost exclusively in the phenomena of transference. It is on this field that the victory must be won—the victory whose expression is the permanent cure of the neurosis."[17]

The cure of psychoanalysis is achieved when patients truly understand their projection onto the therapist; when they do so, they can gain insight into themselves and their relationships to others. When a patient becomes more aware of threatening feelings, he no longer has to defend against them by projection or any other means. He can become more accepting of his whole self and expand his self-knowledge. By understanding and removing the patient's projections onto the analyst, Freud believed that the patient would have a more realistic view of himself and more satisfying relations with others.

Freud saw projection exclusively as a mechanism of defense, a way that we can keep aspects of ourselves outside of our awareness. But like most defense mechanisms, projection is really self-defeating. It is only in the short run that we are protected by projection. Instead of being threatened by an internal factor, we fear an external one. The paranoid spares himself self-criticism but must endure the imagined criticism of others; the phobic is protected from the knowledge that he possesses a dangerous instinctual impulse but sees danger all around him; and the person with delusional jealousy is protected from feelings of faithlessness but sees a partner who is always having or wanting to have an affair. Projection simply replaces anxiety with fear and brings the defensive person out of touch with himself and reality.

Projection is not an easy concept to understand or explain, even for a genius like Freud. Throughout his collected works, there are promises that he will explain the concept more clearly and tie up all the loose ends, as when he wrote, "The thorough examination of the process of projection which we have postponed to another occasion will clear up our remaining doubts on this subject."[18] But such an examination never appears. Freud's editors believe that he may have actually written such a paper and that it is among the "missing papers." It appears that whether he wrote it or not, we will not be helped by it.

Freud's theory of projection has proven valuable to social workers, clinical psychologists, and psychiatrists and has been supported by experimental research done by J. Halpern.[19] Through the research, interviews, and questionnaires done for this book, we

have found that projection does not operate only in the perceptions of neurotics and the delusions of paranoids. It is every bit as
present in so-called normal people as in those seeking help. It goes
on in movie theaters, in homes, in offices, and in bedrooms, often
with the same intensity as in a therapist's office. Carl Jung, probably Freud's greatest student, assigned a larger role to projection
than Freud did. Jung also suggested that we can project more
than just painful, unpleasant, or repressed feelings.

Mythic Projection

Freud had hoped that Jung would eventually take over the
leadership of the psychoanalytic movement, but Jung went on to
develop his own theory and method. Freud maintained that
projection was a defense mechanism—a defense against our sexual and aggressive feelings and impulses. When the repression
and projection of these impulses are extreme, we find paranoia,
phobias, and delusional jealousy. But what about those of us who
are aware of our sexuality and aggression, who have none of these
forms of psychopathology? Are our lives free of projection?

Through his work with patients, Jung continued the explora-
tion of the unconscious. Jung's patients tended to be older and
perhaps more successful than Freud's. Many of them were aware
of their sexual and aggressive feelings, were competent, and by
most conventional standards, had nothing to be unhappy about.
And yet many of them felt something missing in their lives, an
emptiness, an absence of meaning.

The Compensatory Nature of the Unconscious

Jung's view of the unconscious is wider than Freud's. He says
that it balances our one-sided, incomplete conscious attitudes.
What we know about ourselves, other people, and the world is almost always unbalanced and out of proportion. If we pay attention to the unconscious—as it shows itself in dreams, for example—we find the compensatory or balancing attitude that makes
our conscious view complete. For example, on one occasion, Jung
was very critical of a patient and berated her. That night he had a
dream that she was on a pedestal and he had to look up so high
that he hurt his neck.[20] Another patient complained of being faint
and lightheaded. Through great struggle, this patient had
achieved much in his life and had just been offered a prestigious
position in a university. Jung pointed out to him that his dreams
were continually of the past, bringing him back to old neighbor-

hoods and friends. The dreams meant that the man should take note of how far he had risen instead of continuing to over-achieve.[21] In these examples, we see that the unconscious attitude compensates or balances a one-sided and incomplete conscious one. Similarly, intellectuals are likely to have dreams with feelings and introverts are likely to have dreams about parties or large gatherings.

Projection of the Shadow

The balancing function of the unconscious is not only evident in our dreams but also in our projections. According to Jung, everything that is unconscious can also be projected.

Because we usually think too well of ourselves, our unconscious compensates and presents our "shadow" side. We can find this shadow in our dreams and find it projected in the world all around us. Where does evil exist? Not in us, to be sure, but in others. When an industrialist describes a union organizer and a union organizer describes an industrialist, what you hear from each sounds remarkably similar. "I am not greedy, self-interested, selfish, uncaring, and malicious; he is."

Jung believed that to the extent that we are unaware of our own shadow side, we will project it. This increases the chance of doing real harm. If we are unconscious of the shadow, we will see it in our neighbor, or in communists, capitalists, blacks, or Jews. We may take drastic action to destroy this evil. Thus Jung warns us to beware of the self-righteous person. Someone who is ignorant of his own shadow side is unable to fully understand or accept himself and will therefore have a hard time understanding or accepting anyone else. He will see awful, wicked people all around him. If we are unaware of our shadow, we are likely to project it. Jung believed that self-knowledge begins with the recognition of our darker side. Such recognition is necessary for humility and tolerance. These two attributes are necessary for human relationships and growth.

Projection of the Archetypes

Jung's thoughts about the shadow are similar to Freud's view of the unconscious, but Jung found that after becoming aware of our darker shadow side, we may open a gateway to the much more favorable collective unconscious. This is because he believed that self-knowledge must begin with the recognition of our imperfections.

We can find evidence for the collective unconscious in our

dreams and in our projections. Jung was struck by the fact that patients who were quite different often described similar dream images. Although these figures appeared in slightly different guises, Jung found that there were a number of basic ones that he encountered again and again. Not only were these images found in dreams but in the mythologies, religions, legends, fairy tales, art, and literature of all peoples throughout the ages. Images such as the hero, the savior, the trickster, the wise old man, the dream boy (animus) and dream girl (anima) were common; he called these the archetypes of the collective unconscious. These images have been occurring to people in virtually all places and at all times and are therefore of a collective rather than an individual nature. Jung says that the archetypes "impress, influence and fascinate us."[22] They hold a tremendous power and energy. Because they are so overwhelming, most of us are not able to be conscious of them. Instead, we project them out into the world, thus finding our unknown selves, our own hidden potential, in other people.

An example of such a mythical or archetypal image is the savior. It is a universal motif. The savior is the one who will lead us from pain and torment, who can transform us and who can take us through the passages of life. The image belongs to all of us. Jung believed that we have the potential to experience an aspect of the savior, but typically we are unconscious of this archetype. We are terrified of our own power, and we therefore project it. Over the centuries and in different cultures, it has been projected onto masked medicine dancers, witch doctors, shamans, gurus, priests, political leaders, doctors, scientists, and psychotherapists. The projection of such an archetype creates a strong emotional bond with the target and invariably distorts and exaggerates the qualities of that person. But such a projection has useful aspects. If we somehow see a doctor as wise, knowing, and healing beyond his actual ability, it may make it easier for him to heal us. And if we are disappointed by the people we project upon, this may provide us with the opportunity to discover the savior in ourselves.

Primitive peoples projected their unconscious contents onto all sorts of animals and objects. As Jung described such early beliefs, "In that stately tree dwells the thunder god; the spring is haunted by the old woman; in that wood the legendary king is buried; near that rock no one may light a fire because it is the abode of a demon...."[23] People have projected archetypal images into the stars (astrology), into cards (tarot), and into Chinese symbols (I Ching). Perhaps the reason many people have found solutions and wisdom in the occult is that they have projected their own solutions in the form of archetypes onto suitable and ambiguous hooks. When the stars offer a solution, it may be due to an unconscious archetype making an appearance as a projection.

Identifying Projections

"Something that strikes me about the object may very well be a real property of the object," said Jung. "But the more subjective and emotional this impression is, the more likely that the property will be a projection."[24] Modern people are no longer likely to project archetypes onto objects and animals, but our relationships to other people swarm with them. When we see someone, how can we tell whether we are projecting? Jung says that the best way to identify a projection is when someone *appears to cause an intense emotion in us.* If we are unconscious of something and project it, the other person appears to exercise great power over us, and we do not recognize the part we play in the construction of the emotion. The emotion can be either negative or positive. There are certainly people we dislike, but when we feel highly irritated or annoyed, we are likely to be projecting. What could be so disturbing about someone else—unless it is a quality we have and cannot accept in ourselves?

Someone can get under our skin not only because of the projection of the shadow but because we can also project positive mythic images onto them. When this happens, it also feels as if we have no control over our emotional response. Just as we blame someone else for the way we feel when we project the shadow, we give credit to other people when favorable images are projected. Projection always involves placing the cause of the emotion in the other—not recognizing one's own part in the relationship. If we project the anima (dream girl) or animus (dream boy), we feel helplessly and hopelessly in love. The emotion is intense; we are out of control; the other is seen as exclusively responsible for the emotion; the other is distorted, exaggerated, misperceived; we are smitten. Such are the results of mythic projection.

Projection and Dreams

When you are asleep, you are unconscious and therefore cannot possibly have a psychological relationship to anyone. Yet while you are asleep, you may think and feel that you are having all sorts of interesting, wonderful, and sometimes frightening relationships. People you know well, strangers, monsters, beautiful men and women appear and interact with each other and with you. We call these dreams. The people in our dreams appear to be quite separate and distinct. As soon as we awake, we realize that we created a set of imaginary relationships. We acknowledge wisely that in our dreams we were really only relating to ourselves, even though the people seemed so real.

"Projections change the world into a replica of one's unknown face. In the last analysis, therefore, they lead to an autocratic or autistic condition in which one dreams a world whose reality is forever unattainable,"[25] Jung wrote. Jung suggests that when we are awake, we are not as awake as we think, and in the light of day, we continue to dream mythic images. Ultimately such a life, without real relationships, begins to feel insubstantial and painful. We do not realize the causes of our pain and discomfort; we only feel disappointed or disinterested in people because they are not what they appeared to be. Our projections begin to dissolve and our world looks shaky.

Dissolution of Projection

The difficult time during which projections break down represents our best opportunity for growth and self-realization. As our projections and illusions fade, we may become aware of the hero, the shadow, the anima or animus within. Jung called this the process of individuation or self-realization. It means expanding our personality to include what was formerly projected. When we are able to dissolve our projections, we can for the first time have real contact with other people without the murky images in between. By withdrawing projections or dissolving them, we simultaneously become aware of others and ourselves.

Jung believed that it is extremely difficult to be conscious of our projections if we are isolated from other people. If our relations to others are difficult and full of projection, going off to the top of a mountain is not likely to make them improve. It is by being in the world that we can best learn to discriminate ourselves from them. By seeing what affects us, moves us, irritates and amazes us in others, we can find our own true nature.

Often, however, when projections dissolve and we have the best opportunity for a relationship free from illusion, we flee the relationship and search for other hooks upon which to hang our projections. When it seems there is no one left to believe in and we are not ready to believe in ourselves, our archetypes float about, neither externalized as projections nor internalized and incorporated into ourselves. This condition often brings people to psychotherapists.

Transference and Projection

Jung says quite clearly that the patient's emotional attachment to the psychotherapist, called the transference, is a projection. Like Freud, he believed that resolving, working through, or dissolving the patient's projections onto the therapist constituted the most important aspect of the therapeutic work. The patient's projections often provoke counterprojections on the part of the therapist. This is why Jung feels that it is most important for the therapist to have attained some basic self-knowledge. If this hasn't been attained, he operates like a surgeon without clean hands. If the therapist has some self-understanding, he should be able to show the patient that many of his present feelings for the therapist are derived from past experience.

Once this is accomplished, many patients feel content and are able to have successful relationships and careers. Many others, however, still seem to feel a lack of meaning in their lives and may then project archetypal images onto the therapist. They may see the therapist as a hero, or savior, or dream lover. The therapist cannot possibly live up to such expectations. This can cause the patient to experience great disappointment and even hatred for the therapist. Jung would sometimes encourage such patients to join a traditional religion, because most religions have suitable hooks for mythical images. A therapist is simply not as good a target for the projection of the savior image or the shadow, for example, as Christ or the devil. Sadly, as we know, most religious systems today are not capable of holding our projections—our psychology has changed over the last several hundred years, and our religious systems have not. Therefore, many of Jung's patients who dissolved the transference by participating in a religious system became disillusioned and fell back into the transference. For such patients, Jung felt that the long struggle toward self-realization was necessary.

When Jung said, "If the transference is dissolved all that projected energy falls back into the subject, and he is then in possession of the treasure which formerly, in the transference, had simply been wasted."[26] He did not believe that becoming conscious of the archetypes meant that we come to think of ourselves as heroes or saviors. If we say, "I am Christ," or Superman, or the devil, we have been taken over by the image; we have not inter-

nalized it. We do, however, share these archetypes with human-
kind, and to recognize this connection to all peoples from all times
brings with it a deeply felt experience of meaning.

Jungian psychology has not received attention equal to that
given to Freudian theory. Jung's interest in spiritualism, religion, alchemy, and other "nonscientific" topics has not endeared
him to most psychologists. Yet he is certainly a major figure, and
his ideas on projection deserve consideration. Jung perceived
himself as a student of Freud and said in his autobiography that
he did not reject Freud's work but rather built on it. We can see
this in Jung's work on projection. Jung, like Freud, sees
projection as serving a defensive function. People regard as external what they are unable to experience as internal. To feel a
sexual or aggressive impulse may threaten the self-image, so it is
repressed and projected outward. Similarly, to experience the
hero or savior within may be a shattering experience, so that, too,
is defensively projected outward. The difference between Freud
and Jung is more in terms of the content of the projection rather
than the function it serves. Jung's view of the unconscious is
wider than Freud's and so, therefore, is his view of what we are
likely to project.

In the chapters on entertainment, politics, and the news, we
rely more on Jung's approach to projection. People use public figures and celebrities as targets for archetypal or mythic projections. As we move closer to home—job and families—we see all
three types of projection operating simultaneously.

Projection is not an easy concept to understand. The theory is
rich and interesting, but its translation into our daily life is not
an easy one to make. What we want to do in this book is twofold:
first, to acquaint you with the theory of projection, to introduce
you to Jung's work and to aspects of Freudian theory which you
may not be familiar with. Our other purpose is to show the preva-
lence of projection in our lives, to show how much it influences the
course of our relationships.

3
Parents and Children

A most fundamental process between parents and children is socialization. It is hard, slow work for all family members, with much pleasure and also much pain. Its goal is to achieve the independence of the child.

Human beings have a longer childhood by far than any other animal. And there is recent evidence to show that this period is becoming even longer in our culture. The independence of the child and the separation of parents and children are the ultimate goals of socialization. We are not simply speaking of physical distance. Leaving home physically can be a symbol of leaving home emotionally; it may be an indication of emotional separation but it is certainly no guarantee of it. If a grown child cannot talk to his parents, he is not separated from them; he is not truly independent. When a child is capable of caring for himself and can maintain an attitude of understanding and acceptance toward his parents, socialization has probably been completed. However, a great many people never achieve this kind of emotional independence. The reason that many are unsuccessful in their attempts to become truly autonomous adults is that they are unable to break from the projections the parents have had on them and unable to let go of their projections upon their parents. These crisscrossing projections hold the family in a certain locked pattern. Socialization can never be completed until these projections are dissolved and the patterns they make are broken.

Parallel Projections

Parenting is very hard work. Anyone who has been up all night changing, feeding, and comforting an infant knows this. Anything that makes this work a little easier, that helps to strengthen the bond between parent and child, is helpful. If a child looks or acts similar to or seems to have the personality of the parent, the parent may feel encouraged to devote time or pay attention to the baby. We use parallel projection to create this feeling of similarity, which leads to identification with the child. The parent sees in the child his or her own conscious attitudes, beliefs, qualities, and characteristics: "She has my mouth"; "He has my sense of humor"; "She has my temper"; "He has my musical ability"; "She has my coordination"; and so on. The child is a chip off the old block. When we project our own qualities, we are not aware that we are doing so. We may project aspects of ourselves that we are conscious of, but we do it unconsciously.

Like all three types of projection, parallel projection generates problems, because parents do not see the space between themselves and their children. Because it forces the child to become an extension of the parents' ego, parallel projection can delay or even sabotage the growing process toward independence.

As we discussed in Chapter 2, there are two possible reasons for such projections, and they both portend trouble for the entire family. One explanation for parallel projection is that some parents may simply assume that their own preferences for baseball, Republicans, sparkling clean bathrooms, Scotch, and higher education must be shared by everyone and certainly by their children. The other explanation is that parallel projection serves a defensive function. To see any other person as truly different from us is threatening—our ideas and values are called into question. Since most of us are unable to project our conscious qualities successfully onto everyone—we recognize that people are somewhat different from us—we desperately want our home and family to be a place of security and friendliness, with no tension and conflict. Parallel projection banishes all differences. Whether it is true or untrue, saying, "My children are basically like me," helps maintain a sense of security.

When parents use parallel projection, they force their children into the position of defending and protecting them. Children who are often thought of as being the protected in the parent-child relationship become the protectors. They become a buffer between the parents and a different and potentially threatening world. Differences between people make our world interesting, yet most of us are so insecure that we find differences to be threatening. We argue and struggle with people to convince them to see things our way. Even when they don't, we sometimes convince ourselves that they do.

Many people who have not accomplished much in their lives project their own lack of success onto their children. By seeing their children as unsuccessful, they feel that they have not been surpassed. On the other hand, accomplished and successful parents sometimes project excessive abilities onto their children. They see talent, intelligence, and creativity that go way beyond reality. The child may then stretch himself in order to contain these projections, which may cause the child to grow and develop or, if the projections are well beyond the child's ability, there will be much disappointment for both parents and child.

Nature ensures that people are unique. We all are different from one another. This is why parallel projections straitjacket a child. No matter how much of a chip off the old block a child is, he or she cannot be just like the parent. When parents project in this way, the child is forced into a position to which he or she is not perfectly suited. If he accepts the projections, he is not living according to his nature and has given up his autonomy. If he rejects the projections, he is seen as being stubborn, uncooperative, unreasonable, and rebellious. Sometimes such rebellion is necessary in order to be freed from the ties of projection.

Arthur is a physician who has been widowed since his daughter was five. He always wanted her to study medicine but felt that he was not forcing this profession on her. He believed Leslie was "born to be a surgeon." She had her first stethoscope when she was two years old, and he allowed her, even encouraged her, to play in his office. Arthur said he was not "pushing." Every time she asked a question, he pointed out how curious and scientific she was. When she got upset, Arthur would see it as a sign of caring and compassion. If she was unaffected by some difficulty or tragedy, Arthur saw it as detachment. "She was cool and calm." There was no question but that medicine was her calling.

Leslie did very well in school. Her father worked with her and provided her with lots of stimulation and opportunities. Then, in her second year of college (she was only seventeen, having skipped a grade), she said she was going to take some time off for herself. She said she was confused and didn't know what she wanted. Leslie hitchhiked out west and joined a religious group.

Arthur was beside himself with grief. He tried bullying (threatening to remove her), manipulating by guilt (said she was killing him), and bribery (offer her a new car) in order to get her back to school, but he was not successful.

A therapist advised Arthur to make a small contribution to his daughter's religious group. Arthur balked and then he fought, but he eventually sent fifty dollars—no strings attached. The therapist argued that Leslie was asserting her right to independence, to be freed from Arthur's projections. The small donation, to be used as the group saw fit, indicated his willingness to accept and support her even if she wasn't his mirror image. Over time, their communication improved, and Leslie did go back to school, although she studied English literature instead of medicine.

Parents' projections force children into molds that sometimes require great force to break. Arthur forced Leslie into being his replica. Perhaps because of the unexpected loss of his wife, he had an especially great need for the security provided by seeing his daughter as being like himself. Leslie's desire for independence was strong enough to enable her to break out of the projections, but she could not do so piecemeal. She had to rebel. Fortunately they were both open enough to establish contact on new ground: Arthur let go of the projections and Leslie gave up the rebellion.

Family systems involve many levels of projection, which interweave to form a particular pattern of relating. In the following case, we see that what happens when a child does *not* receive parallel projections from his parents can be as important as what happens when he does.

Luther and Dorothy Hughes named their first two children Luther and Dorothy. It is certainly not uncommon for a male child to be named after the father. When this is done, it often sets the stage for parallel projections. "Junior" is expected to take after but not surpass his father. The child is seen as a diminutive mirror image. It is less common for a daughter to be named after her mother, and most unusual for both children to be named after both parents.

Luther and Dorothy Senior had a poor relationship, but they maintained peace and harmony in the family by allying themselves with their children of the same name. Big Luther saw little Luther as being just like himself. The two were a team. They watched TV together and went fishing together whenever they could. Big and little Dorothy did chores, cooked, and played together. This sort of family structure is seriously impaired. There is no couple system, because Mr. and Mrs. Hughes barely spoke to each other; no sibling system, since little Luther and Dorothy ignored each other; and no parent system—the children each had an ally rather than a parent.

The flaws in the family system did not really show, but we could predict that as the children got older and prepared to move out, many problems would surface.

What actually happened, though, to disrupt this system of projections was that another child was born. They could not possibly name him after one of them, so he was called Jeffrey. Jeffrey was seen as being unlike either parent. He was in trouble from the moment he began school, and by the time he was seven, he was getting migraine headaches. The parents had so completely projected themselves onto little Luther and little Dorothy that there was just no room for Jeffrey.

Jeffrey and the entire family were helped by a family therapist who essentially directed Mr. and Mrs. Hughes to pay more attention to each other, forcing them to be more of a couple and to act more like parents. The parallel projections onto Luther and Dorothy Junior had to be dissolved so that the parents could act more responsibly toward all their children. Jeffrey's problems occurred because, while the other children received parallel projections, he became the target for unconscious hostile projections, thus forcing him into the position of scapegoat.

Unconscious Projections

In the late 1800s, the goal of psychologists was to examine conscious experience carefully. Introspectionists, as these early psychologists were called, trained themselves and others to describe precisely the nature of "stickiness," or "blue," or "surprise." They believed that when all the elements of consciousness were described, the task of psychology would be completed. Freud, of course, changed all this by demonstrating that what is conscious is only a small part of our psychology. What we do, he showed, is motivated by forces largely outside of our awareness; he introduced the concept of the unconscious.

Many feelings, impulses, and thoughts that are too painful for us to be conscious of are repressed, but this material does not disappear just because it is outside of our awareness. It causes us to do, think, and feel things we cannot account for: "I wonder what came over me"; "I don't understand why I feel so nervous or sad"; "Why do I keep getting into awful relationships or keep forgetting my child's name?" Freud would say that we are often pushed and pulled by forces out of our awareness.

Much of what is repressed can be found in our projections onto our children. Such projections result not only in psychological but also in physical harm.

Child Abuse

The most serious and harmful result of a parent projecting unconscious material onto a child is child abuse. For thousands of years, parents have been following the Old Testament dictum, Spare the rod and spoil the child. There has always been child abuse, and it is not diminishing. In the late 1800s, "dead or abandoned infants were almost commonplace on city streets. As late as 1892, 200 foundlings and 100 dead infants were found on the streets of New York alone."[1]

Today child abuse has been described as reaching epidemic proportions. This may be because we now have better and more reliable statistics. But no matter how good current statistics are, researchers still believe that for every known case of physical abuse, there are one hundred unknown or unreported cases. The evidence so far indicates that the abused child is likely to be less than one year old, and almost all are less than five. Twenty-five percent of all fractures seen in children under the age of two are caused by child abuse. It is estimated that between 1973 and 1982, there were 1½ million reports of abuse, with three hundred thousand permanent injuries and fifty thousand deaths. The causes of this continuing horror are complex.

What the numbers represent in human suffering is difficult to think about. We present these figures quite purposefully, because ignoring the facts has been an important part of the problem. Most of us have a tendency to think of children as their parents' property, to be treated as they see fit. We also tend to think that good parenting is instinctive—that anyone can do it with little or no preparation, training, or education. As a result, we deny that the problem exists. We tend to look the other way, choosing to believe that if there is child abuse, it is decreasing. It is not.

Recently a picture has begun to emerge in which it looks as though child abuse is caused by parents' projections. Here are some of the facts as they were reviewed by Blair and Rita Justice.[2] Abusing parents are just as likely to be men or women (fathers abuse slightly more than mothers, but mothers are more likely to commit serious abuse), and child abuse occurs throughout the social classes. Abusing parents are not as a rule either crazy or cruel. In fact, they love their children. They do tend to be under more stress than parents who do not abuse their children. Abusing parents have been found to experience a prolonged series of unpredictable changes such as divorce, loss of a job, sickness, pregnancy, a son or daughter leaving home, sex difficulties, someone beginning or ending work. These changes can cause a tremendous desire to be taken care of. The parents desperately desire to be parented, and they act as children themselves. Therefore, they project the image of a parent onto the child! Child abusers have never grown up. They were never properly taken care of as children, and most were in fact abused themselves. As adults, they are frustrated, angry, and still wanting to be cared for.

Abusing parents tend to form symbiotic relationships and depend excessively on each other rather than on themselves to meet their needs. They tend to have few friends outside of their marriage. They are passive, denying their own ability to take care of themselves, and they attempt to demand or manipulate the partner into taking care of them. In other words, abusing parents, as a result of not being properly parented themselves, want their partner to be a parent. The partner is unable to accommodate or cooperate, because the partner, too, is looking for a parent. Both parents, now under stress, unsatisfied and frustrated, look to the remaining member of the family to fill these needs. They come to expect the child to take care of them instead of vice versa.

Research reveals that such parents have unrealistic expectations of their child and expect him to be a source of comfort and nurturance. These parents treat the child as though he is much older than he really is. The parents project the image of a parent onto the child, who is simply too young to understand what is wanted and unable to respond appropriately. When people, even children, are unable to hold our projections, we become disappointed and frustrated. A small child is quite obviously an improper target for the projection of the parent. The frustrated parent strikes out at what seems to them the most obvious cause of their distress—a crying, defenseless child.

Child abuse is the most obvious and serious result of parents' unconscious projections. Such projections actually are more likely to result in psychological rather than physical harm, and it is also more typical to see parents harming children with no conscious realization that they are doing so. This can be seen in several case studies that follow.

Triangulation and Unconscious Projections

Even when couples care deeply for each other, they make mistakes and often become anxious and irritable. There are problems and disagreements about sex, money, friends, how to spend time,

and so on. Although this is not pleasant, it seems to be even less
desirable when they ignore or deny feelings that could result in a
marital conflict. We have found, from our own surveys and questionnaires, that couples often deny having troubles or conflicts. It
is astonishing to see how many couples say they are *very* happy,
very satisfied with their partners and their relationships. When
spouses are also parents, there is the danger that denying conflicts will draw the child into the conflict.

Triangulation sounds like *strangulation,* and this is what happens when a child is drawn into a conflict that properly belongs to
the parents. An unhappy triangle is formed when painful or unacceptable emotions the couple has in their relationship are denied and projected onto the child. The child then becomes a scapegoat. As long as the parents are angry at, disciplining, and
fretting over the "problem child," their attention is focused away
from their own problems and onto their child. It is sometimes easier to have problem children than a problem marriage, and such
children are created by unconscious projections. In the following
case, we can see how not one but each of the children took turns
being troublesome in order to keep the parents from facing a very
serious problem of their own.

As the Wilson family came into the room and met their family
therapist, they seemed to be unsure as to what to expect. They
seated themselves in a horseshoe pattern, with the therapist sitting opposite them at the open end of the semicircle. At one end
was the smallest girl, Diana, and on the other side was the mother,
Rita. Closer to center was Cal, who was twelve. Butch was between
Mother and Father. At the rear was Paul, the father.

Paul
(Father)

Cal	Butch (Problem Child)
age 12	age 11
Diana	Rita
age 7	(Mother)

Therapist

The therapist asked why the family had come. Butch, it seems,
was having problems in school. He was behind in both reading

and math and was thought by his teacher not to be working up to his potential. Mr. and Mrs. Wilson took turns expressing their concern about Butch. They were worried about him and had even been paying a private tutor as well as a therapist, who was treating Butch individually.

Butch minimized the problem. "I'll be okay," he said. "I'm just having trouble with that long division, and my new teacher doesn't explain things good." As the therapy session unfolded, it was revealed that a few years ago, Cal, the older brother, saw a guidance counselor about problems he had been having in school. Diana had been wetting the bed a year earlier than that, when she was six.

All through the therapy session, the parents did not once express any concern about themselves, each other, or their relationship. But the therapist noticed in their standard medical history that Paul, the father, had a kidney problem. She asked if that presented any problems for the family. Butch began to cough, and Cal reached over and poked him. The mother disciplined the two boys, and the topic of the discussion quickly shifted from Father's illness to concern about the children. This one incident reveals the sequence of actions that is causing the problems in the family. Paul has a serious medical problem and denies it. His wife may at some point have to tend an ill, incapacitated husband and have sole responsibility for her family. She denies this. These are not easy things to contemplate, but rather than worry about themselves, they project their worries onto their children.

Children are good targets for parental projections. They do not have fully established identities. They are receptive hooks for just about anything parents want to hang on them. If you project important traits or attitudes onto adults, there is always a good possibility that they will not accept them and become your projection. If you feel scapegoated at work, you may try to defend yourself and speak up for who you think you really are, or you may leave and find another job. Children don't quite have the ability to defend themselves; they have fewer choices, and so often they struggle to become what is projected onto them, even if it sometimes means getting sick. Chances are if you believe a child to be bright and industrious, he will be. If you see a child as a failure or as having problems, he will cooperate. Children are receptive; they soak up everything around them—including their parents' projections.

In the Wilson family, the parents were afraid to worry about themselves so they worried about their children. When children are seen as having problems, they do. The pattern of projection in this family is a protective one. The parents protect themselves from confronting a potential horror by being concerned about much more manageable problems. The feelings and emotions involved with such issues as serious illness and death are so painful and intense that only a "problem child" can distract the parents. A "problem child" also gives the parents a convenient outlet to explain their tensions and their conflicts. Even the way they arranged themselves around the table revealed how Father, sitting in the middle, was being protected. And when the therapist asked about the illness, the whole family cooperated and changed the subject.

In this case, the therapist was successful in getting the parents to recognize their projections. She gradually and skillfully encouraged the children and Mother to talk about their worries about their father. Later, the family talked about their concerns for their mother. The children did, of course, express much sadness and worry about their parents. Once this was allowed to be expressed and to come out into the open, and once the parents were able to experience their own fears and sadness, they no longer had to project them onto their children. As the parents talked more to each other, the children were freed from the projections and their "problems" worked themselves out.

A Legacy of Unconscious Projections

Psychologists of all theoretical persuasions recognize that who and what we are is determined to a great extent by our family of origin. Escape is impossible. And yet we know so little about our family, our parents and grandparents. Americans seem to be especially ignorant of their family history. Who we are as individuals, our successes and problems, are often a result of what has been projected onto us. We play a part in a larger drama. We cannot possibly be free of what has been projected onto us unless we understand that larger drama.

In order to unravel the projections that are passed down through the generations, some therapists make genograms.[3] These are charts or spatial representations of the family of origin, usually beginning with the grandparents. What were your grandparents like? How was their marriage? Who was dominant in the marriage? What were the rules in the family? Then on to your parents.

Why do you think your parents married? What did they expect

from each other when they married? What did they get from each other, and what did they not get? Among your parents and aunts and uncles, who is most favored by each of the grandparents? What did someone have to do to please or displease a parent? What kind of sex life do your parents have?

By carefully mapping a client's family with names, dates, notes, facts, alliances, and expectations, some therapists hope to find the context for their client's problems. Current conflicts are linked to past conflicts. They are perpetuated and expanded through the projections you have received and the way you project upon others. The genogram is a tool that has as one of its uses the identification of the patterns of projection.

The following case study illustrates the continuation of unresolved conflicts over more than one generation. These problems are "inherited" through the process of projection.

Jerry is forty-one years old. He has a healthy family; an attractive, devoted, and capable wife; and is a reasonably successful professional—a dentist with his own office—yet he is quite unhappy. Looking into mouths day after day truly bores him. He constantly fantasizes about buying a medical building and getting dentists to work for him so he can stop doing dentistry himself. He also has fantasies about striking out for himself and leaving his wife and children. It is not that such thoughts are uncommon, but Jerry tortures himself with them. He stays up nights planning and designing the dental offices. During the day, however, he does almost nothing to actualize his plans.

Jerry's grandfather, Jerome, whom Jerry was named for, owned a small business but was a gambler. Jerry's father, Peter, told him how his grandfather would come home with presents for everyone on the days he won and wouldn't come home at all on the days he lost. Over time, he lost more regularly than he won and began drinking heavily. Then one day he went to work and never came home again.

Peter survived, became a lawyer, and acted with considerable caution throughout his life. Although his own father's desertion caused him much pain, he named his first child after him. Jerry's problems and conflicts as an adult seem quite understandable in view of his family history. That his father named him after his own father symbolizes the fact that Peter projected many of the qualities he saw in his father onto his son. At the same time, Peter instilled in his child his own more cautious nature. Perhaps Peter was trying to undo with his son what his own father had done. He was hoping to create a Jerry who would be more stable and would not run off.

The conflicting projections that Jerry has received have resulted in his own inner conflict. He has carried the weight of a set of projections that properly belong to his grandfather. Because his father persisted in seeing in him the qualities he hated and feared in his own father, Jerry has been molded in a certain way. On the other hand, Peter also taught him to respect stability, perseverance, and dependability. These two sets of expectations met and clashed in Jerry. He is unsure of who he is—his father's father or his father's son.

Understanding the conflict—and therefore the projections—that have been passed down to us by our family can be a useful way of understanding our current problems.

Mythic Projection: The Magical Child

When we see our children, we not only project our images of ourselves or our worries or the repressed feelings that properly belong to our mate or our parents; sometimes we see something quite different, something quite extraordinary. Our child appears almost too wonderful and miraculous to be true. This image of the magical child is of a mythical nature and has always been projected by parents onto their children.

The symbol of the child god or Christ child can be found in many different mythologies and religious systems. The earliest Christian mystics had visions of radiant children. We all know of folk tales with elves and dwarves—magical little people. In all these legends, fairy tales, folk stories, and religions, the child, in the words of Saint Christopher, is "smaller than small, and bigger than big." The magical child is thus exposed and vulnerable, almost insignificant, it is so small; and yet it is divinely powerful, invincible.[4]

We see contrary or paradoxical qualities when we project the image of the magical child. We see our child as completely dependent, vulnerable, weak, innocent, powerless. This expression can create the most nurturing, supportive, and protective feelings in a parent. And yet the child is unbelievably powerful. He can manipulate us, master himself and the world around him, grow, change, learn, give an adult a feeling of meaning in life. No wonder he is "smaller than small and bigger than big."

Most parents experience a powerful love for their children and can well understand some of the feelings we have just described, but many still have the good sense not to treat their children as small gods. They are not gods. Yet why do some of us act as if they were? Carl Jung believed that as adults, we sometimes progress too fast and move ahead in such a way that we lose touch with ourselves and our past. In order to get ahead in our careers, we ignore other aspects of ourselves and become excessively one-sided. Often we become completely unchildlike. We lose our imagination, our spontaneity, our sense of joy. We become artificial. Whenever we become too one-sided in our conscious life, the unconscious builds up a strong counterposition in order to compensate for this extreme imbalance. Therefore, people who lose their childlike nature may have dreams about magical children or be fascinated by stories, myths and legends about magical children, dwarves, or elves. They often will project the image of a magical child onto a real child, most often their own.

When this happens, the child is distorted by the projections and changed into the parents' unknown and longed-for wholeness. The god-child becomes a symbol instead of a reality. The symbol represents the future and the potential to grow, change, and become complete. This symbol is a unity of opposites—big and small, weak and powerful, masculine and feminine, innocent and wise. Instead of having a relationship with a small human being, we project our wholeness onto the child and transform him into a mythical symbol. It is difficult for us to become "as little children," so we deny the child in us and create child gods around us.

The consequences of this type of projection are many and complex. Parents who feel that their children are wonderful and special give the child the important gifts of confidence and high self-esteem. If parents are able to control their feelings and emotions and provide discipline along with instilling this sense of self-worth, the child can work at growing into the projection and become the image that the parent perceives. However, there is a real danger that children who are seen as small gods may simply be spoiled.

The child who receives mythical projections from the parents may not be too popular around the neighborhood or in school. This child can be arrogant, obnoxious, and selfish. The child may also come to rely too much on the parents for his self-esteem and the maintenance of this false image. Of course, eventually all children must separate from parents, and separation from this projection

50 PROJECTIONS

can be especially painful. The child learns that he is not a god and must find a satisfying human life for himself. Parents may become disappointed and disillusioned if the child becomes ordinary instead of extraordinary. Sometimes in order to prove to parents that they are not gods—in order to break free from these powerful projections—children may take drastic measures that are destructive to themselves. Having problems or getting into trouble is a way for a child to convince his parents that he is human.

The Problems of Adolescence

Adolescence is the time when the whole set of parental projections—parallel, unconscious, and mythic—commonly begins to break down. The bonds that are formed by parental projections are pulled and stretched around the time the child enters adolescence, because this is when the child is expected to break away from these bonds. But the separation cannot be truly successful as long as the child is tied to the parents by projection.

Everyone knows that adolescence is a very difficult time, but most people believe that the difficulties are strictly in the adolescent. However, just as the child is moving into a new life stage, so too are the parents. If you think about the most stressful times in your life, you may find that they occurred when someone entered or left the family system, at the time of a death, a divorce, a separation, or a birth. When these events happen, everyone and everything changes. Such enormous change causes stress for all the family members. We can see this in the following case study.

The Cooper family entered therapy with a male and female co-therapist. Family therapists often work in teams, so no member of the couple feels outnumbered. The father began by saying that their only child, Chris, a sixteen-year-old daughter, was driving him crazy. She was nasty, angry, failing in school, and staying out late, sometimes not coming home until the next day. He said that his wife would be extremely upset when their daughter didn't come home. She demanded that he be disciplinarian. He reported that he "had smacked Chris around quite a few times but it doesn't do any good." The situation at home was so bad that he said softly, "I just wish sometimes that I didn't have to come home."

Mrs. Cooper was furious at Chris and during the whole first therapy session appeared livid with anger. She said that her daughter was ruining their lives. The mother reported that she was completely ineffective and had no control over Chris, which is why she had to get the father to administer the punishment.

This case presents the familiar story of a girl who is leaving home before she is really ready, and who, therefore, is not really going anywhere. It also shows us how parental projections maintain a tie that should have begun to be reexamined and loosened. What are the parents projecting onto her that causes so much trouble?

Jay Haley, an innovative family therapist, once wrote that if you listen carefully to parents complain about a problem child, you can hear them complaining about each other.[5] The Coopers have serious marital problems. Rather than face these problems, they projected their dissatisfactions onto their adolescent daughter. Although Chris believes she is trying to break out of this unhappy family, in fact she is doing the opposite by acting the way she does. By misbehaving, she has cooperated with her parents and sacrificed herself in order to spare them the discomfort and pain of facing each other.

If we look at the impact upon the daughter that her own actions have, we can see this process. The mother is a very angry woman. The father feels like leaving (he, of course, is really capable of leaving the family). So what happens? Father is not upset with Mother for being angry, nor is Mother upset with Father for wanting to leave. They both see their daughter as someone who is angry and running off and therefore the cause of their problems. They need to see their daughter as troublesome in order to protect themselves and their marriage. By projecting their dissatisfaction onto their daughter in this way, there is another curious benefit to the marriage. The daughter is such a problem that Mother *has* to have the father around to be the authority and disciplinarian. The end result is this: daughter's problem helps Mother draw Father back into the family; daughter's problem keeps Father from running off.

Of course, when parents project onto a child in this way, they are not at all aware that they are doing so. They would say that they don't want their daughter to be such a problem and that *she* is creating stress and tension in the marriage, not decreasing it, but this is not completely true. It is often less threatening to see a child rather than a mate as the source of one's problems. The parents project their troubles onto her, and she, the good daughter, accepts. When adolescents leave home prematurely, they often get into trouble. The parents then worry, and the old network of projections stays intact.

Parents see in their children an image of themselves, a source of security and protection. They also see aspects of themselves of which they are unaware, which may create a child who is troublesome but who serves a protective function as well. Children often help keep parents from painful feelings about themselves, each other, or their own parents. Parents also project a mythical image that gives meaning to their lives. How can parents easily allow a child who serves so many functions to grow up, develop an identity, become autonomous, and leave? Of course, most parents *do* want what is ultimately best for their children and do struggle to let go of their projections, but it is not an easy task.

If a person runs away from home or stays out all night, he or she has not made a successful separation. More often, such a leave-taking makes certain that parents will be more involved, more worried and concerned—the projections in the family will be unchanged. Physically leaving is not the same thing as psychologically leaving. Many young adults can live at home with their parents and be quite autonomous and independent, whereas others may leave home but are always asking for financial help or often getting into trouble.

There are, of course, many other problems common to adolescence besides running away. These include failing in school, not getting or keeping a job, taking drugs or alcohol, becoming eccentric, being depressed or aggressive, winding up in a jail or hospital. The proportion of adolescents suffering nervous breakdowns or going to jail is higher than in the rest of the population. Jay Haley, in his new book *Leaving Home,* reasons that all these types of failures and problems lead to the same result—the family organization can remain unchanged.[6] The parents can still focus their lives on the child.

Family Therapy with Adolescents

Traditional psychotherapy with problem adolescents disregarded the parents and worked only with the adolescent. Psychoanalysts sought to enable the adolescent to reach greater self-insight and understanding. Behavior therapists worked to reinforce appropriate and adaptive behavior and to remove or extinguish the problem behaviors. Such traditional approaches don't take into account the fact that an individual adolescent's problem can only exist in a context, usually a family context. What good does it do to change thoughts or behaviors in an adolescent if the parents continue to project onto the child?

Most family therapists refuse to work only with a problem adolescent. They see the entire family because they believe that an individual's problem is part of a larger family problem. Instead of changing the adolescent, they work to change or restructure the entire family.

Family therapists attempt to dissolve projections in a family in numerous ways. The therapist may ask the husband and wife to talk with each other and agree on what is expected of the child and decide on what to do to encourage the child to set limits or to decide together about appropriate punishment. The parents of the problem adolescent have a very difficult time making such agreements. They undermine each other and perpetuate the problem. The therapist can *force* the parents to focus on each other and on their disagreements and can help them to agree and cooperate on a strategy to help their child. This process encourages the parents to see each other more clearly and to stop mixing up their own difficulties with the child's. If a family therapist helps a family allow the adolescent to succeed and leave home, it is almost inevitable that the parents will become aware of their own problems and the problems in the relationship that the child kept them from facing. Family therapy with an adolescent, when it is successful, almost always leads to a freeing of the child and eventual work or therapy with the couple.

Children's Projections

The relationship between parents and children is confusing not only because of parents' projections onto the children but because the projections are just as strong moving in the other direction. We spend so many years living intimately with our parents, and yet most of us know very little about them. R.D. Laing said, "The first family to interest me was my own. I still know less about it than I know about many other families."[7] This is true for most adults.

When we were young, we wanted and needed our parents to take care of us, to provide for us, comfort us, play with us, and keep us amused. We also needed them to heal all our physical and emotional wounds, to sense when we were disappointed, and, in fact, to know us better than we knew ourselves—to read our minds. We also needed our parents to set limits and to provide discipline. Without limits, we would not have a structure and a sense of security that comes from knowing clearly what is permitted and what is not. Without limits, we would not be properly prepared and equipped for the real world and we would resent our parents for it. We needed our parents not only to provide for our basic needs and for setting limits, we also needed them to give us room for autonomy and independence. We needed to find things out for ourselves—to explore and experiment in order to develop a sense of confidence and self-esteem. If a parent does too much for a child or sets limits that are too rigid, children learn to not trust themselves and their own judgments.

It is clear that it is not easy to be a good parent and it is impossible to be a perfect one. Yet many children think that their parents are perfect. This projection of the mythical perfect parent figure can work when we are young children. Parents can kiss a bump or bruise and make it better and often do know exactly what to do to make a child happy.

Some children refuse to allow these projections to dissolve and cling tightly to the notion that their parents are perfect. They refuse to see any faults or weakness; they refuse to recognize their own ambivalence. They maintain a childish view of themselves, their parents, and the world. Psychological research has shown that adults who idealize their parents tend to dislike Jews, blacks, and other minority groups.[8] Why should there be this connection? It may be that people who idealize their parents have to deny any negative feeling toward them—any feelings of annoyance or dissatisfaction. But such feelings are inevitable and they do not disappear. They go underground and appear conveniently projected onto minority groups. It seems that if we are better able to see some faults in our parents, to recognize our own mixed feelings for them, we do not have to project all our negative feelings onto minority groups. If we idealize our parents, we turn them into one-dimensional images of perfection and then balance this by turning certain groups into one-dimensional images of evil.

Many of us, by the time we reach adolescence, do begin to feel annoyance and dissatisfaction with our parents. We want to break free from their projections. This is also the beginning of the breakdown of the perfect-parent projection. Like most projection breakdowns, it is accompanied by feelings of disillusionment. Real people peek out from the veils of our projections with strengths and weaknesses. We don't want real people as parents and condemn them if they are not perfect. When projections break down, we almost always blame the target for not adequately carrying the projection. Our parents don't only seem imperfect to us, they seem boring, incompetent, selfish, overbearing, and the like.

The dissolution of the perfect parental projection is part of the adolescent rebellion. Such a rebellion can lay the groundwork for a new, more genuine relationship between a parent and child. The rebellion becomes a transformation as parent and child are freed from their projections. They can develop a sense of mutual love and respect without idealizing each other. They can see each other's faults and weaknesses and still accept each other.

All too often, unfortunately, the adolescent rebellion continues into adulthood without transformation. In such cases, the child never gets over the disappointment that came when the projections dissolved. The child (now an adult) still wants and needs a perfect parent and will accept no less. Therefore the parents are never accepted but only blamed. This phenomenon of grown children blaming their parents for not carrying their projections has been encouraged by many psychologists. If you have problems, the Freudians suggest, it is because your parents were too repressive; the Rogerians, because your parents were not accepting enough; and the behaviorists, because your parents didn't provide the right environment.

Psychologists too need scapegoats, and often client and therapist form an alliance with the parent as scapegoat. We are sometimes astounded to hear and see therapeutic sessions in which a fifty-year-old client and the therapist are discussing the ways in which the client has been damaged by his or her parents. As long as we blame our parents for not holding our projections—for not being perfect—we can never see them clearly, and what's more, an unresolved relationship with our parents will inevitably be carried over into our dealings with other adults.

4
Couples

In the not-too distant past, the expectation was that once a man and woman married, they were joined for life. Divorce was not only discouraged, it was considered by most to be a socially unacceptable solution to marital problems. Couples were expected to work things out as best they could, to preserve their marriage at all cost.

In some circles, the pendulum has swung to the opposite extreme. Couples in relationships of long standing are considered escapists, hiding from the "real world" of outside interests and other relationships. Therapists who refer to themselves not as marriage counselors but as divorce counselors expect their clients to follow a new social norm—serial monogamy.

Between these two extremes lies a new middle path of greatly increased freedom. For most of us, there exists a wide range of choices to make about our primary relationships—a spectrum of alternatives that can be extremely anxiety-provoking. The norms are blurred; blueprints for life are increasingly chaotic or nonexistent—to marry or live together, to have children or not, to remain monogamous or not, to work out marital problems or simply throw out the relationship and start again. In the face of these choices, with decreasing emphasis on "saving the marriage," more and more couples opt to end their relationships. It is a well-documented fact that American couples are having trouble staying together. In 1981, there were well over a million divorces (5 for every 10 marriages), with the divorce rate continuing to climb. And these statistics don't even include the dissolution of the relationships of unmarried couples.

Of course, the freedom to divorce has a positive aspect. It is a road out for men and women who in other times would have been trapped in conflict and hostility. For a couple who have explored their relationship and found it seriously lacking or harmful, who have spent the time and energy to accurately assess their situation, divorce is a positive step. Research suggests that people are better off divorced than unhappily married, but research also shows that we are better off happily married than divorced.

It is well known that the effects of divorce are devastating. Almost always it has serious negative consequences for children.[1] The breaking up of a marriage is one of the most stressful events that can occur in our lives, disrupting the basic functions of eating and sleeping. Studies have shown it to be strongly associated with mental illness (especially for men), car accidents, physical diseases, suicide, and death by homicide.[2] If we divorce, we are almost surely in for a very hard time. Sometimes this difficult path is a necessary one to take. But what is really unfortunate and troubling is that many of us choose this drastic step without ever really getting to know our partner. We fall in love with a fantasy we have and become disillusioned when our fantasies fade. We divorce in anger and disappointment, doomed to repeat the same mistake in another relationship if we don't come to an understanding of what went wrong.

The existence of conflict in a relationship—even serious conflict—is not necessarily a clear sign that the relationship should be ended. That we find ourselves wrestling with problems can be a signal not that our relationship is dying but that it is growing. When we are in the throes of a painful time, we can often lose sight of this simple but important fact. As we work our way through conflict, we are shedding our illusions—our projections. This is likely to be a painful process, but its resolution has the potential for bringing a great deal of joy. Keeping this in mind can spur us on to find solutions to our problems.

In order to examine the projection process in couples, we interviewed several dozen people and distributed six hundred questionnaires to men and women throughout the country. One hundred ten people aged nineteen to eighty-one in a great variety of occupations responded to our survey. We wanted to know the most serious problems that couples faced. Our respondents, whose average age was forty and who were involved in their relationship for an average of fourteen years, indicated the following "top ten problems" (listed in order of importance):

1. differences in frequency of sexual desire
2. conflicts over what is seen as important in life
3. insufficient sharing, affection, communication

4. differences in how to spend time
5. conflicts due to stressful work affecting the relationship
6. differences in how to spend money
7. dissatisfaction with (sexual) foreplay
8. conflicts over attending to career and attending to relationship
9. conflicts over friendships with other people
10. relationship seems boring

We found statistical evidence that showed that couples who try to solve their problems by "talking about alternate solutions . . . in a fairly systematic way" tended to be most satisfied with their relationships and partners, whereas couples who spoke strictly on an emotional or feeling level tended to be less happy in their relationships. When we feel our emotions have taken over, gaining full control of us, this signals that projection is at work or breaking down. A good relationship depends on the sharing of feelings, but when the predominant ones are blame and anger, the relationship is not helped if these are consistently expressed.

In couples, we found the operation of all three levels of projection—parallel, unconscious, and mythic. In this chapter, we discuss all three. The breakdown of the mythic projection of the anima/animus is so serious and misunderstood that it will be treated separately in the next chapter.

Parallel Projection

When two people begin life together as a couple, there are certain types of problems that typically arise early on. They commonly find themselves arguing about how they will spend money, when and whether to marry, whether to have children, how to divide responsibilities, what is or is not really important in life.

These early conflicts have a common root—the realization that the two of you are not of one soul and mind. Perhaps this seems an obvious fact, but most often when we fall in love, this simple truth gets lost in the tremendous shuffle. Our needs and desires create distortion, magnifying and minimizing various qualities in our lovers. We so much need someone to share our lives that we tend to assume our partner understands and indeed shares our world view. It has been demonstrated over and over again in psychological experiments that the old adage that opposites attract usually doesn't hold true. Most of us find similarity attractive, and we tend to be drawn to those people we think share our values. Another old saw, Birds of a feather flock together, accurately describes this situation.[3]

A common misreading of our partner's qualities, the exaggeration of compatibility, is a good example of parallel projection. The person we think we are, the sum of all things that we consciously know about ourselves, is projected onto our partners during the early phases of courtship and romance.

The results of our survey showed that many people enter into relationships and simply assume basic similarities where none exist. Sometimes differences were perceived but dismissed much too quickly with the thought or fantasy that the other person would soon change and be more similar.

Libby and Don

"Don is an extremely independent person," wrote Libby, who is twenty-nine years old. "He does have some trouble sharing. Sometimes I feel like I direct the relationship, like if I didn't ask anything of him, he would give nothing. When we first started going out a year and a half ago, I fell in love with his kindness and gentleness. I suppose I also loved listening to him play his music. He writes, plays, and sings, and he is a joy to watch. When we moved in together, I was sure our relationship would build, that gradually we would develop a mutual dependency, but now I am beginning to see that it's not working out that way.

"I need a general sense or direction to head in. I'm not obsessed with this, but I am conscious of time marching on (childbearing age in particular). Sometimes I feel like I'm waiting for him. I have verbally and as nonthreateningly as possible confronted him with what I need as well as where I see him—his fears and resistances. I feel I have to set some timetables for myself— maybe a year. I need to know if we are going to be a couple with children, if he's going to be part of my future or not. I'd be happy to hear an alternate compromise, but I can't wait forever. Maybe I'm too focused on this relationship. I figure he has about a year to decide."

"I played rock 'n' roll with a popular band," Don wrote, "but the hip life-style caused me to pack the guitar away and spend more time writing, publishing, and doing work in the studio. I love Libby very much. She's a very intelligent, very beautiful woman who (because of her experiences in life) knows and understands my unorthodox behavior and life-style. She allows me to be me and lets me know that I am loved for that reason. There are a lot of different things that make our relationship great; one of them is sex. She's very good at sex and so am I.

"About six months ago, more than a year after we started to live together, a pretty big problem came to the surface. Libby started to sound like she wanted the American dream—children, a home, two cars. She didn't admit to all of this, but now and then she would get cranky and critical, and when I drew her out, the American dream appeared. I made it clear that I did not long for these things. Our society has outgrown the need for a couple to remain together forever like in colonial times. I told Libby about my feelings; there's no sense in either of us living in a fantasy. Today's interest rates make it crazy to buy a house, and I can't ever see having children. There is no sense in fooling ourselves; we've got a great thing going, just the two of us, and we're going to keep it that way. I really think she understands and accepts this and our relationship as it is."

According to Libby, the most serious conflicts in their relationship are: "Conflicts over what is seen as important in life," "disagreement about when or whether to have children," and "conflicts between attending to career and attending to relationship." According to Don, the conflicts about children were a problem but aren't now. He sees their most pressing problem as "conflict due to stressful work affecting the relationship."

It seems clear that these two people recognize that they are having some problems, but they do not agree on how serious the problems are or even what they are.

Don tells us that he made it clear to Libby that he will never want a house and a family. She apparently hasn't heard this. Perhaps she feels he will change over time. Maybe his nonverbal communication indicates more flexibility than his overt verbal remarks. It seems to us that she is seeing the possibility of similarity that isn't there.

Libby says she "can't wait forever" and that she has "confronted him." It looks to us as if she plans on leaving within a year if she doesn't get what she wants. Don, it seems, hasn't heard this at all.

What they both need desperately is someone to share their values, to be like them. Since this is not apparently the case, they have made each other up. Much of what they believe about the other comes from their own projections and is not part of the other person at all.

Sam and Beverly

Parallel projection is not inversely related to age. One would think that as we get older, we would have less of a tendency to assume naively that someone else thinks, acts, or feels like us. Our research indicates that this is not the case.

Sam Blacker, seventy-two years old, is a retired schoolteacher. He was married to his first wife for twenty-five years, and they had two children, both now adults. Sam's first wife died of cancer when she was just fifty, and three years later he met Beverly. Sam recalled:

"I was just coming out of a depression when we met. I wasn't seriously interested in getting married again, but Beverly is a very attractive woman, and when we started going out to movies and shows, I felt very attracted to her. One of the things I missed most about not being married was sex. My first wife and I did it all the time, and I thought Beverly would be a great partner. She was in very good shape, and we even played tennis together several times a week. We are from a generation where no one expects sex without marriage, so it didn't surprise me that Beverly made it clear that she didn't want to have sex. I just assumed that once we got married, things would really change. Unfortunately they didn't. This is the biggest problem in our marriage, which has lasted seventeen years. I always get the impression that sex for her is a duty and not a joy. I have tried to resolve this problem by discussion and by trying to arouse her passion, but this has failed. I must say, however, that she tries to please me but just doesn't know how even though I explain what she should do. At our age, I suppose this isn't supposed to be an important issue, but it is. My first wife was so good in this area, and I was so sure that Beverly would be as good or better that I haven't gotten over the disappointment."

Parallel projection runs rampant in sexuality. J. Halpern and Mark Sherman discovered in their research, described in *Afterplay*,[4] that many people simply assumed that their partners liked what they liked after sex. Time and again people would say things like, "Afterplay—doesn't everyone just sleep?" or "We clean up after sex just like everyone else." Of course, we discovered that not everyone sleeps or cleans up, but a great many people think that others do as they do; that is, they use parallel projection.

Probably the factor that is most responsible for these projections taking place around sex is a lack of discussion and direct communication. Even after the sexual revolution, many of us are still reluctant to talk with our partners about sex. Maybe because of performance anxiety, fear of rejection, fear of getting too close or involved, we don't talk about our likes and dislikes openly. Since an easy place to project is onto a blank screen, the lack of open and honest communication makes the possibility of projection more likely. The less we know about the feelings of our partner, the more we might assume that the other's needs are the same as ours. All through the courtship, Sam assumed that Beverly desired as much sexual contact as he. He entered into marriage assuming a similarity that did not exist, and he is suffering because of it.

Dr. Ralph Stern

Intelligence, like age, is no defense against parallel projection. One man we interviewed, who presented one of the clearest examples we have ever seen of parallel projection, is a well-respected psychiatrist. Dr. Ralph Stern met his first wife while he was traveling to South America, examining ruins of early cultures. Dr. Stern did not speak Spanish and the woman of his dreams did not speak English, yet (or perhaps more accurately, therefore) they fell in love. All the doctor's friends advised him to wait until they got to know each other before rushing headlong into marriage, but Ralph would not have it so. He was sure their love could conquer any problem. It didn't. As they got to know each other, they realized they had almost nothing in common. He told us that about a month after they married, he watched her watching cartoons on television one Saturday morning, and he threw up all afternoon. A few months later, they were divorced.

Ralph was very aware of how lonely he felt while traveling in Europe several years after his divorce. He was staying with friends in Brussels when he met Bernice. Ralph remembered a smattering of his high school French and Bernice spoke almost no English. They had a marvelous romance. Ralph's friends often acted as interpreters, and the foursome went out frequently and laughed a lot together. Somehow Ralph returned to the States unmarried. He held off, but it was clear that he planned to return to Brussels, marry Bernice, and settle down back in the USA. Virtually all Ralph's friends urged him not to do it, to wait, pehaps to visit Bernice for a longer period of time. In her, he said he saw his soul mate—a woman he could talk with, be with, and laugh with. They spent so much time laughing together, he was sure he wasn't overestimating their compatibility. He was. They married, came to the United States, and were divorced in less than a year.

Although most of us do not succumb to such extremes of parallel projection, exaggeration of similarities is really much more common than we may realize. As the realization begins to dawn on us that we don't share as much in common as we once thought, conflicts begin to arise. What is happening is that the projection of our conscious selves is breaking down. We see that the person we thought we knew is not the person we are living with, that our partner (thank God) is not our clone. Example: you thought your partner felt as you did—that furniture was more important than expensive vacations; that it's more fun to go out for an evening than to watch TV; that housecleaning once a month is sufficient. You begin to find out that you were wrong about these and any number of daily items.

As these problems arise, it is possible to keep the parallel projections going by not listening to the partner. There are many complex and ingenious strategies of nonlistening. If a problem is brought to our attention, we can: (1) deny it; (2) act dumb; (3) change the subject; (4) make a joke; (5) punish our partner or start a fight; (6) have sex; (7) call our partner crazy or paranoid.

1. *He:* I don't think we have enough sharing and communication in our relationship.
   She: How can you say that!

2. *She:* I don't like it that you spend so much time at the office.
   He: What do you mean by *so* much time?

3. *He:* I'm concerned that you might be interested in another man.
   She: I made a very special dinner for us tonight.

4. *She:* I would like more closeness after sex.
   He: Afterplay is for theatergoers—ha ha ha!

5. *He:* I didn't like the way you spoke to my mother.
   She: If she didn't call all the damn time, you wouldn't have to worry about it.

6. *She:* I feel you've been very intolerant and angry with me lately.
   He: Let's go to bed and I'll show you you're wrong.

7. *He:* Since I lost my job I don't think you respect me as much
   as you used to.
   She: You must be crazy.

In every one of the foregoing vignettes, we see how easy it is to
avoid or evade our partners' concerns. These could all be considered "silencing strategies"—ways to keep conflicts and problems
hidden by manipulating the partner to shut up. These strategies
can take us years to master, and we can become so good at them
that we usually don't even know that we are using them.

Resolving Parallel Projections

Carl Rogers, founder of client-centered psychotherapy, has
suggested a simple formula for improving communication in his
book *On Becoming a Person.*[5] We think his suggestions can help
to resolve the problems caused by parallel projection. When two
people are having a conflict or argument, Rogers suggests that before stating one's own position, one should *restate the other's position, to the other's satisfaction.* If both people agree to do this,
they will be forced really to listen to and understand the other
point of view. Parallel projections then become impossible.

If Libby and Don employed this technique when they were
talking about buying a house or having a child—if each had to
carefully restate the other position—they would be much more
likely to perceive the other's position and perhaps even to understand their differences. As it now stands, they are poles apart but
don't even know it. It is impossible to resolve differences unless
they are first acknowledged. Of course for Rogers's method to be
useful, both parties must agree to try it. If one person, in the middle of a fight, says, "Let's use Carl Rogers's suggestion," and the
other says, "That's just more of your manipulative psychological
nonsense," Rogers's approach probably won't work. However,
where there is a willingness to hear the other's point of view and
to dissolve the projections, the technique can be highly effective.

Projecting Parental Images:
Unconscious Projection

Understanding intimate conflicts would be simple if we only assumed that our partners were just like us, but relationships and
conflicts are considerably more confusing than that.

Not only do we project what we are conscious of, but we also project the contents of the unconscious. At every stage in life, we greatly overemphasize our own self-awareness. Surely we know now how much more aware and developed we are than we were, say, seven years ago. But seven years from now, we will be likely to have a similar point of view about our past. To the extent that many aspects of ourselves are undeveloped and unconscious, they can be projected onto our lovers.

Many of these unconscious images are likely to revolve around our parents. For many adults, their thoughts and feelings about their parents remain unresolved and unclear. As we all know, the relationship between parent and child is tremendously complex and intense. These contaminated relationships inevitably affect our dealings with other adults, especially our most intimate relationships.

In order for new marriages and families to begin and thrive, there must be a separation from the family of origin. When this has not happened, problems will inevitably occur in the marriage.

Nick

Nick, a postal worker, thirty-two years old, wrote, "The fact that one year after getting married, my wife bought a house with her mother without consulting me tells the story. I have had to live with not only her mother but her grandfather, too. This arrangement has caused great stress, disharmony, and hostility between us. We never had any privacy. She shares all the bills with her mother. They go shopping together, play cards, talk about everything, etc. It's sick! I've gotten so turned off to her that I've started to have sex with other women."

Gwen

Another respondent, Gwen, age twenty-eight, wrote about her five-year marriage with a policeman. Her story had a happier ending.

"His mother offered us an apartment attached to her house before we got married. It was neat and clean, inexpensive. I didn't think it was a good idea but he said we agreed to do it and we already told her we would live there. It was a terrible mistake. We were constantly arguing about his mother. She interfered with our relationship to no end. It was the most horrible experience in my whole life. It all ended with a physical fight. We hurt each other quite a bit, and I got the worst of it. I gave him a clear alternative. It was either move out or divorce. We moved. This is now

the happiest time in my life. We are finally living a life of our
own. We do a lot of sports together: hike, jog, bicycle ride, etc.
We're even talking about having children."

Many adults are simply unable to separate from their parents.
They remain at home, unmarried. In the cases just mentioned, in
spite of the marriage, one of the partners was more concerned
about the original family than the new one. The parent remained
the first love. Some parents develop all sorts of physical and psychological problems to keep a child home. Adults who are unable
to separate fully from parents feel their immaturity. They experience frustration and stagnation. They are also likely to develop serious sexual problems, since their sexual feelings for a partner
threaten their bond to their beloved parent. We saw from the second case that such bonds can be broken even late in adulthood.
This break, however, is not an easy one to accomplish.

While some people stay at home, loyal to one or both parents,
others leave and get married too early. Very often, adolescent
marriages arise because of inadequate parent-child relationships.
The adolescent wants to get out at almost any cost. Physical, emotional, and sexual contact are seized and held onto because the
person is so needy. It is not infrequent that such a person will not
only marry too young but will have a child before being ready to
handle the responsibilities. With a child, the new parent can give
and receive the kind of love that was missing in the original family. But again the person is too needy to be an effective, responsible parent.

Melanie and Mike

Melanie is a thirty-two-year-old secretary who has been married
to Mike for eight years. They have two children, seven and five
years old.

"Mike fulfills the role of the husband and father exceptionally
well. This is unusual, I think, for men of my generation. Mike has
a great respect for me as an individual and is considerate. That's
the good side. The bad side is that he is completely boring and
predictable.

"I married too young, and I really want out of this marriage
and a chance to live my own independent life. My parents had a
terrible relationship. My mother was weak and passive and my father was scary and sometimes violent. Mike is a sensitive man,
very unlike my father, and I really appreciated it. Now I find him

annoying. He is willing to do almost anything at any time. He is so satisfied and easy to please, it's disgusting. I am very energetic, a doer. I didn't consider myself as the dominant person in any relationship before this one. I now find that I have to make all the plans and all the decisions. I have to push him to make plans, take stands, etc. It won't change. He's a nice guy but he just doesn't do it for me anymore. He cannot understand why I feel the way I do. I want to date and see other men (I haven't told him this part yet), and I'm tired of the housewife role. It's just not for me.

"I think I'm not going anywhere until my children are grown. It is not pleasant to wish away years of your life, but sometimes I actually calculate the days. Because of our strong love for our children, we have managed to stay together."

Family therapists have noted that we often choose a mate in order to resolve a problem in our parents' relationship. Melanie saw her mother being abused by an aggressive father and probably selected Mike as a mate to ensure that this would not happen to her. It is also true that the reason people give for why they are unhappy in a marriage is very close to the reason they present for the original attraction. At first, Melanie saw Mike as gentle and sensitive; now she sees him as ineffective. She is transferring or projecting much of the anger she experienced with her parents and their inability to give her what she needed onto Mike.

John and Jill

When John and Jill got married, John said he was most attracted to Jill's warmth, strong feelings, emotions, and loyalty. John probably felt this way because his mother was not a very warm and caring person. Jill's family of origin was very chaotic, and her initial attraction to John was that he seemed stable and nonthreatening. After three years of marriage, John saw Jill's emotionality as hysteria and Jill saw John's stability as uptight, conservative stagnation. They were divorced. What John and Jill missed from their parents they saw in distorted form in their partners. When these projections dissolved, there was nothing left.

The most important gift a parent can give to a child is a feeling of self-worth and self-acceptance. People who received the message that they are worthwhile as children and learned to accept themselves can tolerate criticism and benefit from it. Although other people and their praise are valued, all their actions and feelings are not dependent on the reactions of other people. If we have a mature sense of identity, a clear sense of who and what we are, we do not have to conform or rebel or withdraw. We can tolerate, accept, and value the differences between us and the people around us. We have less need to project.

One woman we interviewed had unusual facial features but was quite attractive. She had often asked if her mother thought she was pretty, to which her mother replied, "To *me* you will always be pretty." This subtle undermining of the daughter's confidence and self-image affected her throughout most of her adult life. If we do not receive acceptance as children, if our self-image is murky and not very positive, we become terribly dependent on other people for our feelings of self-worth and esteem. We have an insatiable need for praise, a need to be liked and accepted by others. Many people devote their lives to avoiding criticism and pleasing others and are destroyed if they don't win approval.

The more the sense of self is chaotic and disorganized, the more there is a lack of self-acceptance, the more we develop an excessive dependency, the more we color and distort the people around us. This is seen in the following case.

Debbie and Joel

When Debbie came into the office, she seemed nervous and uncomfortable. Her eyes darted quickly around the room before she sat down, as if she were making sure there was no one about to attack her. While we talked, she fidgeted with one hand and clutched her bag with the other.

"I don't know what's wrong with Joel and me. It used to be so good.

"My sister fixed us up at first. Joel was a law student, and I was a secretary. I still am, although now I am an executive secretary. On our first date, Joel took me to a lecture given by a well-known lawyer and politician. I didn't understand all that was going on, but I was impressed. I was impressed with the whole business, you know—the law school, the fancy chairs and lights, the speaker, and of course Joel. A lawyer, I thought. What could be bad? My mother always told me that it was just as easy to marry a rich man as a poor one, and although Joel was definitely not rich, I knew he was going to be. He was hardworking and ambitious.

"I know I am very attractive. My whole life men have been trying to, you know, put the make on me. I knew Joel wanted me, but I also knew I wanted much more than sex with him. I wanted a permanent relationship. It was something my mother never had and I wanted it.

"You should see pictures of my mother when she was younger—absolutely gorgeous. I have her eyes and cheekbones. Yet when I was about four years old, my father left. I never really knew what happened and I still don't know. One day I just remember my mother crying at the kitchen table, saying "Daddy's gone." It didn't really bother me then, but later it did. My mother started working, and we saw a lot less of her. I have two sisters— one older and one younger. Ellen, the older one, was almost as much my mother as my mother. She cleaned and cooked and took care of us when we were sick. Mom never talked about Daddy. I think she was just so ashamed and embarrassed.

"When Joel and I started to live together, we had so much fun. We didn't have much money, but it didn't matter. I was making pretty good money, and Joel was going to school during the day and studying nights, but our weekends together were great. We would sometimes spend a whole day in bed, drinking coffee, reading the newspaper, and making love, of course. Joel always seemed to have time for me. We would talk in the morning over coffee before going to work and have nice dinners together. We would sometimes even meet for lunch. I knew that kind of thing doesn't always last so long, but now it's just awful. I don't know what went wrong or why, but all we do is fight.

"Joel works *all the time!* He says he is really trying to establish himself. He works at the law office during the day, and at night, he and his friend do some kind of consulting. I feel like I hardly see him, like I am lowest on his list of priorities. This morning he got up and I asked him if he had time to hear what happened at the office between my best friend at work and the boss. He said he had the time, but before I was finished I could tell he just wanted me to stop and get out of the house. He said, 'Can't you tell me just the gist of it?' I tried to but I could see he wasn't even listening. He was glancing at the clock and looking all around like he couldn't wait to leave. I cried for a half-hour after he left.

"I've even lost him on Saturdays. He works in the morning and then plays racketball in the afternoon. Sundays, our one day together, are spent fighting. We fight about almost everything. Joel doesn't like my sister because she asks him why he doesn't spend more time with me. If Joel is home when she calls—and she calls a couple of times a day—we have a fight. My sister also suggested that maybe I could help Joel with his work, that I could be involved with his new consulting business. Joel said he has to do it on his own. He wanted to really create a business that would be his and his alone.

"One night, after we had been fighting and arguing for what seemed like a few hours, we agreed to try to really help each other. We said maybe we really need to compromise, and we gave each other one wish. My wish was for Joel to spend the morning with me and his wish was that I let him get out of the house and not 'hang on him' every morning. Our idea about giving each other a wish seemed to go noplace. My sister suggested another compromise. She said Joel should have Saturday for himself—it should be his day—while Sunday should be my day, a day we could do things together. Joel didn't seem too thrilled about the idea, and I felt awful. Why does he have to bargain to get out of seeing me? It doesn't seem right at all. I have to give up something in exchange to be with him? What kind of marriage do we have? Certainly not the kind that is going to produce any children."

When two people become a couple, they must learn to express their needs and listen to their partner's needs, and when there are differences, they must learn to compromise. Debbie and her husband Joel are willing to do these things. They are willing to listen to each other and even agree to grant each other a wish. But their wishes are irreconcilable. Joel demands more time to be on his own to develop his business, while Debbie demands more time from him. And yet there is not the slightest indication that either of them is thinking about divorce. Somehow their problems are unsolvable, and somehow the relationship keeps working.

The image Debbie projects is an unconscious one—the father she wants, never had, and never can have. This makes her needs unsatisfiable. This is why compromise can't be effective. The needs are not reasonable; they are based on childhood emotions. The constant contact with her sister also indicates a lack of separation from the family of origin.

Debbie has an especially immature self-image and an inadequate sense of self. She thus resorts to obtaining pity and sympathy from Joel. Her need to be cared for makes her feel even more inadequate and inferior. This in turn instills in Joel a greater sense of guilt, along with the feeling that he should offer even more help and pity. Eventually, of course, Joel in his role as helper has become resentful, exasperated, and exhausted. In time, the stronger person in such a relationship becomes punitive, rejecting, and hurtful and no longer motivated to help but rather to destroy the helpless one.

A woman may look for a substitute father in her husband; a man may look for a substitute mother in his wife. This will create the same patterns of conflict and tension that were in the parent-child relationship.

We did not interview Joel and so we cannot identify the quid pro quo that underlies the marital relationship. What seems to be happening in Joel and Debbie's marriage is that one person is operating with a facade of exaggerated strength and assertion, whereas the other moves into compliance and submission. One person has become superadequate and extremely parental, while the other has become infantile. We can only hypothesize that since they are not even considering separation, Joel needs Debbie to need him as much as she needs him.

Frank and Jan

Jan and Frank have been married for eight years. They began couple therapy because they argue very frequently and in the last year had sex only once. Unlike Debbie and Joel, who had a complementary relationship (one person clearly dominant), Jan and Frank have a symmetrical relationship (no one clearly dominant). It seemed that most of their arguments were not so much about a particular issue as they were about who was in control. This was why they fought about almost everything—how, and how much, money to spend, who did what chores, and so on. Both were determined not to be taken advantage of.

Jan's mother was an extremely responsible woman. She worked full-time while Jan was growing up and yet kept the house spotless, cooked wonderful meals, and took Jan to dance classes and to other cultural events. Sadly, her mother died of cancer when she was just fourteen, and although her father was "an all right sort of fellow," Jan never fully recovered from her loss. In the course of therapy, it was revealed that Jan felt that her mother's early death was caused by her overdeveloped sense of responsibility.

Frank's mother, in contrast to Jan's, was completely irresponsible. She drank, did not work, and didn't even keep the house presentable. Frank always consciously resented his mother and closely allied himself to his father, whom he felt was much taken advantage of.

Somehow these two found each other "like bats in the night." Although they could not see it consciously, they were perfectly matched. Both sought the more responsible opposite-sex parent they had lacked as children. Jan remains loyal to her mother. She will not be taken advantage of and die young as her mother did. She therefore demands that Frank not be as passive as her father. Frank remains loyal to his father and refuses to be taken advantage of by an irresponsible wife. In fact, both Frank and Jan are quite responsible, yet they do not see each other clearly, because each carries an unconscious image of an irresponsible parent of the opposite sex and projects it onto the other.

If we project an unconscious image of a parent onto a spouse, we are actually creating an incestuous relationship. No wonder they do not have sex. They are repulsed by the partner, whom they see (unconsciously) as the parent of the opposite sex. Such dynamics are much more common than is usually believed.

We found from our survey that most couples with sexual problems do not have "technical or mechanical problems." These are the difficulties that the Masters and Johnson technique is so effective with.[6] Problems like orgasmic dysfunction can usually be treated successfully in a two-week intensive program. But our respondents indicated that these aren't the usual problems. It seems that most people know what to do and how to do it but have difficulty synchronizing their desires. This was the problem most often cited by the couples we surveyed. For some reason, whenever one person is desirous, the other isn't. Such problems are not dealt with by adjustment, manipulations, and new sexual techniques. The couple are unable to enjoy each other sexually because they see a fragment of a mate and a piece of a parent. The resulting familial and incestuous experience is a turnoff. The parental images have to be dissolved for the marriage to be fully consummated.

Some of the most difficult conflicts a couple face involve the stress and tension created by work, illness, loss of money, joblessness, or death of a loved one. All these problems are extrinsic to the relationship itself and yet have a tremendous impact. It is at these times that our unconscious parental images are most likely to be projected. Under duress, our need for someone to make things right emerges strongly and affects our perceptions. We need a "mommy" or a "daddy" to care for us. We project these images onto our mate and are then disappointed to find that the projections don't fit.

A stereotypic but still valid example is this: a man comes home after a hard day's work, expecting his wife to be his mother. He wants attention, food, warmth, and comfort on demand and is disappointed and angry if he doesn't get this. His wife, on the other hand, has had just as hard a day with the house and children. She too wants her partner to take care of things and make things right when he comes home.

In most of our other relationships, we control our impulse to project our parental images. But at home, it is almost as if we "let go," regressing and acting like children, hoping our mate will hold the parent projection. Our pent-up frustrations and discomforts are released and spill over. We don't feel we have to control ourselves, so we have tantrums. We think that Mommy or Daddy will always love us no matter what we do. But since our mates are not our parents, they may not. When we expect our partners to be our parents, violence becomes a real possibility. This is because when the projections don't fit, we get very frustrated.

The magnitude of family violence became particularly obvious during the summer heat wave of 1972. Page 1 of the July 22 *New York Times* contained an article describing the increase in murders during the previous few days of extreme heat in New York City and discussed the number of people who had been murdered in the previous six months. On page 2, there was an article totaling the deaths in Northern Ireland during three and a half years of disturbances. About as many people were killed by their relatives in six months in New York City as had been killed in three and a half years of fighting in Ireland.

You are more likely to be killed by a relative than a mugger, a psychopath, or a Russian, and you are most certainly more likely to fight physically with a relative than with anyone else. One legal researcher estimates that more police calls involve family conflict than do calls for all criminal incidents, including murders, rapes, nonfamily assaults, robberies, and muggings. Recent estimates suggest that 56 percent of couples have used physical force on each other.[7]

If we find ourselves clashing repeatedly with our mates when one or both of us is under high external pressure, our first task is to separate our internal from our external conflicts. We often admit that we are short-tempered and irritable with our partner when outside problems crowd in. But why should this be so? If we examine the conflicts of these stressful periods, we can see that they are caused by unrealistically high expectations of competence from our partner. Our projection of the parent figure onto them is an expression of our need for help with difficult circumstances. But there is no perfect parent capable of carrying our projections. We become frustrated and angry. Our partner is not a suitable hook for our projections and is not the perfect parent who will help us.

By projecting these images, not only are we damaging our relationship, we are also greatly decreasing our ability to deal effectively with the problems at hand. We are only creating other problems. If we can extricate the energy used up in these battles, we free ourselves to deal competently with the external issue, be it illness, financial difficulty, or whatever other obstacle presents itself. We can also strengthen our relationship by working together to cope with the external problems. In order to do this, we must find a time when the storm has abated somewhat, a time of relative calm in which to discuss the situation. By working on dissolving the projections, we can improve the quality of our relationship. By directing our energy outward to the problem rather than inward to our partner, we surely must be more effective in handling our difficulties. What happens is that we find ourselves becoming more competent—becoming the parent we sought in the other.

Projecting the Dream Boy/Dream Girl

One of the most significant contributions made by C. G. Jung was to suggest that deep in the unconscious, beneath the layers of forgotten childhood memories, lies our undeveloped potential, which is expressed in the form of images. For Jung, then, there is more than unresolved childhood dilemmas to project. We may also see in someone else just those very positive qualities that we have not actualized in ourselves. We may meet our undeveloped potential in someone else and long for that person. This longing may symbolize our desire for wholeness and completion.

There is a very special and unique phase of many couples' relationship—the initial head-over-heels-in-love feeling, which has been celebrated since time immemorial in song, verse, art. Most of us have been fortunate enough to be swept up in this whirlwind, and most of us also know that it is rare for this intensely romantic period to last for very long.

What are the dynamics behind this magical time? Why does it end? The fact that this phase is often described as *paradise* and *extraordinary* is an indication that there is an unreal relationship—not between two people but between a person and his or her projection.

Within each of us exists our opposite. In each man, there is a feminine aspect of his nature, and within each woman exists the masculine. Sleeping within our own unconscious is this perfect man or woman, waiting to be awakened. When a woman meets an appropriate man, this unconscious perfect figure is projected onto him. To the extent that she is seeing the "dream boy" rather than a real person, the relationship is illusion, infused with the magical quality of a fairy tale.

Although the relationship is illusory, it feels wonderful. Not only have you found your dream, but there is a person who thinks *you* are a "dream." And in some ways, you are both right, for you are in fact dreaming, or making each other up. Although this might be delightful for a while, it is really an autistic or masturbatory relationship—a relationship with yourself rather than with another person. In some way, we recognize that our intense feelings about the other person are not completely real, because we sense that others are threatening. Early in the relationship, there are not only value conflicts brought about by the breakdown of parallel projection but also conflicts involving other people. This is because any outsider can disrupt or disturb the flattering mutual system of projections. Old friends and relatives will just not think of you or your lover as a god or goddess and will not act in such a way as to support your images of each other. Thus in these early stages, there can be conflicts about relatives, in-laws, friends. One or both members of the relationship often can be irrationally frightened by the possibility of having children.

If we are not ourselves involved in an intensely romantic relationship, we may find the actions of new lovers to be somewhat obnoxious. Here we see two ordinary people acting as though they see each other as extraordinary. They have little time or energy for us, only for each other. They make each other feel extraspecial and other people extraneous. This is clearly the honeymoon period, and many couples are not only separated from other people psychologically, but they also make a physical break.

Projecting the dream boy/girl image does not cause severe problems in a couple's relationship; it postpones them. Eventually all honeymoons end, and we have to face another real person rather than a flawless being. It is the breakdown of these projections that can cause more serious conflicts, as we shall see in the next chapter.

5

Loss of Love

For some couples, the honeymoon period is quite long-lasting. The survey and interviews revealed that there are people who hold onto their illusions for a surprisingly long time. Others lose hold of them very quickly. They've scarcely swept away the wedding rice before they must deal with the debris that is created as their dream projections slip away. Though the timing varies, what appears to be invariable is that sooner or later, we begin to see discrepancies between our dream figure and the real person with whom we are sharing our life. And again and again, people report that this process of discovery and change is a frightening one. We are waking from a dream to face reality; we struggle to keep our eyes closed but we can't. To confront a real person who lives apart from wishes, expectations, and projections has been reported as difficult by virtually all the people we have surveyed.

The Suitability of the Target

There are many factors that can combine to determine when the awakening begins and how quickly it progresses. Crucial to the timing is the "fit" between the projection and the target. Sometimes our partner actually possesses very few of the anima or animus qualities. The clothes of the dream figure fit so badly that the person underneath soon stands revealed. In such a case, people usually become disappointed relatively early on, feeling foolish as their friends say, "I never could see what you saw in him."

How could we make such a mistake to begin with? Physical appearance plays a very important role in determining the suitability of the target figure and the timing of the projection breakdown. There seems to be no doubt that we are most likely to project the anima or animus figure onto a physically attractive person. Good looks count for a great deal in our society. The importance we place on appearance is very high. In one social-psychological experiment after another, it has been shown that physical appearance more than any other factor determines whether and to what extent we are attracted to someone.*

It seems quite clear that when it comes to focusing on a target for our dream boy or girl, we are quite likely to choose someone who is good-looking whether or not the person is suitable, that is, whether or not there is a congruence between the surface appearance and the underlying personality. We find it easy to think of the person in wondrous ways, to see in him or her a whole manner of positive, desirable qualities. But though it may be love at first sight, disenchantment follows quickly when there is little beauty below the surface.

Just as it is exciting to fall in love with a beautiful personification of our dreams, it is extremely pleasurable to be thought of as such a personification. As we all know, there are clear advantages to being attractive. But what might not be quite so obvious is the

---

* Experiments have demonstrated that from early in our lives, beauty strongly influences our opinions of other people. A study of nursery-school children showed that even at an early age, they tended to like their classmates who were attractive rather than those who were unattractive.[1] Even adult evaluations of children are determined largely on the basis of appearance. One researcher had women read reports on serious classroom problems that were supposedly written by teachers.[2] With each report was attached a photo of the child who was said to be the culprit. When the child was attractive, the women tended to be more lenient in their evaluation of their problems. When the child pictured was unattractive, the evaluators tended to view the child as having more serious personality problems, sometimes even suggesting that professional help was required.

When it comes to relationships between the sexes, physical appearance is a powerful factor—not only in the way we think and feel about someone but in how much we value a person's opinions of us. We place more value upon the beautiful than the ugly. There is clear empirical verification of this from a number of experiments. In one, a beautiful woman posed as a graduate student in clinical psychology. In the first part of the experiment, she was made to look quite unattractive. In this guise, she interviewed several male college students. At the end of the interview, she gave each subject what was reputedly her clinical evaluation of him. Half of them were given good evaluations, half very poor ones. She repeated this process with another group, with the only difference being that she looked beautiful. The impact of this change was great. When she was unattractive, the men were not very affected by her opinions. Both those who were evaluated well and those who were evaluated poorly liked her moderately well. However, in the attractive condition, her impact was much greater. Those men who received good reports liked her a great deal. Those who received poor reports disliked her a great deal. However, they wanted the opportunity to come back for another evaluation.[3]

fact that there are also real dangers. Very attractive people lacking equally attractive personalities find themselves not only the source of admiration and desire but also of disappointment. Experiencing the quick withdrawal of the dream projection is very depressing. For a while, we are wrapped in the dazzling garments of a fairy-tale being, and then quickly we are stripped of them. Although people generally attribute happiness to attractive people, such a generalization is quite absurd. Being the object of disappointment and rejection leads to great self-disappointment and disapproval. When no effort is made to develop the inner person, this experience of being desired and rejected is likely to recur, bringing greater pain with each repetition. In the course of the survey, a number of cases were encountered in which attractive people were not disappointed in their partners but were disappointments to others and thus disappointments to themselves.

Of course, we are not all attracted to each other exclusively on the basis of outward appearances. Almost every relationship involves some mixture of accurate perception and projection. Some of us are better able to look beyond the superficial, to begin relationships that are partially free of projection, and based on accurate recognition and assessment of the other.

Life experience and conscious development will play roles in determining the extent to which a relationship is dependent on projection as its basis. The less it has been initiated and sustained by the projection of the dream figure, the longer it can continue untouched by its breakdown. In those instances in which there are two relatively conscious people engaged in a relationship of substance rather than fantasy, it may take quite some time for the problems of projection breakdown to become apparent. But our research indicates that at every stage in life, people tend to overestimate their self-awareness and to underestimate the amount of projection in their relationships. Everyone interviewed in the early stage of a relationship said that although they were aware that many relationships were superficial and doomed to failure, theirs was "real."

Delaying Tactics

No matter how good the fit between the dream projection and the real person, sooner or later the differences will make themselves apparent. This process is inevitable. As wonderful as a lover might be, he or she is not a mythic personage. We cannot live with people without beginning to note discrepancies between who we thought they were and who they are. So the breakdown of the dream projection is a process all of us in primary relationships must live through.

The establishment of a bond with another human being is a primary need all members of our species share. This bond helps us feel "grounded" in the world, secure. When we begin to perceive the real person peeping out from behind our projected image, we see a stranger. Most of us are unaware of our role in creating our vision of our partner and are equally unaware of our role in its dissolution. As in any new or changed situation people tend to experience discomfort and even fear.

This process of change is a gradual one. In its initial stages, people note relatively small discrepancies between their projection and reality. These could be referred to as cracks in the image, and the initial strategy at their appearance is to try to fill them in. The survey and interviews uncovered a variety of ingenious strategies people use to patch up the picture. A typical move at this point is to make small requests of the person in order to bring him or her back in line with the projection. "Could you please stop drinking so much coffee (beer, or supply your own pet weakness)?" "I'm sure you'd really love skiing. You're a natural athlete and you'd enjoy spending more time outside." "You might look nice in a pair of designer jeans." "Would you change your golf plans and go to the new gallery with me?"

Asking our partner to be more like our ideal can certainly be a positive move. When we are asked to change our behavior or expand our interest, we are motivated to grow, to move in a new direction in an attempt to fill a projected image. If the move is successful, you have augmented and enriched yourself. You are rising to the occasion of the demand. In so doing, both you and your partner benefit. This positive result is most likely to occur when there is a relatively good fit between the projection and the person. In such a case, the person need only stretch to fit this new area—he or she possesses the potential to meet the need. When there is a poor fit, a more drastic move is required—perhaps more transformation than expansion. In such a case, this strategy is likely to be unsuccessful. Both partners are disappointed and disillusioned. The requesting partner is upset when his wishes are not met, making the discrepancies clearer. The partner being asked to change is disturbed by the sudden apprehension that he is no longer regarded as flawless.

At this stage (and even at later stages) of a relationship, requests of our partner often take the unexpected form of gifts. Sometimes we offer a present to our dream person and not to our partner. It is often something we wished they wanted. It is what we want them to want. One couple we interviewed was very extravagant on their first anniversary. The presents they exchanged were wonderful; unfortunately they were also completely inappropriate. Susan bought John a flute because she "knew he really secretly wanted to devote a lot of time to learning an instrument. But he'd never spend the money himself." John gave Susan a pair of downhill skis and a down jacket. The fact that she had never skied or even expressed an interest in doing so didn't stop him for a moment. After the initial excitement, the trying on and tentative playing, the presents lay untouched. They were offerings to gods; the real people had no use for them. They were demands in the form of gifts—please be this way, do this, be more athletic, musical, sensitive . . . be more like the person I thought you were.

It would seem that if the target can't be changed to ensure a good fit, then perhaps the projection can be. Unfortunately this too is a difficult task. Dream figures have remained unchanged through the centuries. As long as our projection of this figure remains unconscious, we cannot will it to change. Like a nighttime dream, it is an unconscious fantasy. We wield as little control over its existence as we do over dreams. But many psychologists have found that dreams can be changed. If we think about them when we wake, if we examine them, feel them, live them consciously, we can influence the direction our dream life follows; so too with projections. As we will see at the end of this chapter, the way to change their control over us is to "own" them, to become conscious of their existence in our relationships.

As illusion (dream boy/girl) and reality (real person) get more out of phase—as the cracks become wider—couples employ other strategies in the struggle to keep the projection process going. If much energy is directed outside the relationship in job, career, or family, it may be possible to sustain these ideal images for longer periods. There are simply fewer opportunities for projection and real person to clash. If a couple is consumed exclusively with making money, raising children, or pursuing careers, it may be much later in life that they confront the breakdown of their dream projections.

As our projection of the dream figure begins to give way in the face of daily reality, we experience a great discomfort and discontent. Sometimes this malaise is felt as a lack. This is indeed accurate, for we are lacking or missing our dream figure, or at least some parts of it. If we are unaware of the source of our discontent, we may interpret it as a need to get a better job, have children, buy a home, move to the country or to the city. Instead of attending to each other, the couple directs attention outward in an attempt to delay the time at which the awakening begins.

The survey and interviews indicated that sometimes intense "nest-building" immediately precedes the breakup of a marriage. Buying, building, or renovating a home is often an all-consuming affair. Both people find themselves totally absorbed with furnaces, carpet samples, stripping floors, calling carpenters—occupied with endless decisions and details. When the last worker leaves or the last piece of furniture is delivered, some couples are left with a feeling of desolation. They once again have to face each other. It's as though there's a feverish attempt to enclose the relationship in a perfect cocoon, to hold it together from the outside. Unfortunately this often doesn't work. A viable union between two people must be sustained by its own inner strength, not propped up by an exterior shell.

Whichever stalling tactic is used, however, the projections do finally break down. A whole complex of discordant emotions rises up as this occurs. The partner who is withdrawing the dream projection feels angry and remote from the other, often being highly intolerant. He or she often perceives the partner as possessive or confining. They not only begin to see someone with weaknesses, faults, and failings; these traits are also exaggerated, just as similarities and positive qualities were initially overestimated. Attributes that were once accepted and even admired are now experienced as annoying. The partner from whom the projections are being withdrawn may feel very bewildered. Many people express feelings of insecurity. They complain about insufficient sharing, lack of affection, and poor communication. Jealousy often figures quite prominently.

The Dream Breaks Down: Anne

Anne seemed confused and searching for something as she spoke about Charles and the pain she was in. "We were married seven years ago, and I guess I may have been too young. I was twenty and had been on my own for about a year. We met at a rally against the war. This was at Berkeley, where we both were on scholarship. There were thousands of people there. A friend introduced us. He called a few days later, and we started to go out. It's hard for me to imagine this right now, but at that time I loved everything about him—the way he lit up and smoked his cigarettes, the way he moved, the way smoke came out of his nose and mouth when he talked. He seemed to have a strong moral sense of justice and injustice, and he impressed people—including me— when he talked about politics. We were both seeing other people, and when he didn't call me for a week, I decided to take the situation into my own hands. I called him and told him I missed seeing him and invited him over to dinner. It was a special evening, and a few months later we were married.

"Four years ago, we had Billy, and even then I already knew things weren't right. I think I may have gotten pregnant trying to protect our marriage. Charles was always talking about how we didn't have enough money. We do, you know, but all through my pregnancy he was saying things like, 'Cribs cost so much money' and 'The hospital bills are highway robbery' and 'Doctors should be killed or at least soundly beaten.' Here I was having our baby and he was talking about medicine in other cultures and the advantages of socialized medical care. It's not that I disagreed with what he was saying. It's just that there is a time and a place for it. He seemed unwilling to be involved in the emotions of having a child or dealing with my needs.

"Since Billy's birth, I feel like I don't want anything to do with Charles. I have sex with him because I feel it's an obligation, but I don't find it satisfying. I don't like the way it feels when he touches me, so how can I possibly reach orgasm?

"Two years ago, I went back to graduate school to finish my degree in sociology. A woman comes to the house to sit for Billy while I am gone. My husband says I spend too much time in my studies and not enough time with him. I think that happened as an escape. He also says that I should stop going to school and get a job since we need the money. How can he want me to get a job and at the same time spend more time with him? It's a contradiction. I think he's really just jealous about the friends I've made at school. I have both male and female friends, and he thinks I spend too much time with them. When we discuss this, he exaggerates the amount of time I'm with them and tells me he feels neglected. When I invite them over, I always try to make him feel like one of the group and ask him to do things with us, but it hasn't worked.

"Lately things have gotten very horrible. I try to avoid him. My stomach sinks when I come home and he is there. He is often angry and picks on little things I do almost constantly. When I try to have any kind of discussion with him, he resorts to shouting, arguing, and trying to make me look bad. I haven't been able to tell Charles about how horrible I feel, and I certainly haven't been able to tell him about Frank. At first, my relationship with Frank was strictly sexual. I really think it was my husband's treatment of me that led to this affair. But now Frank seems to mean a lot more than just a sex partner.

"A few months ago, I tried talking to Charles about the possibility of separating. I told him I felt confused and needed the time and space to work things out for myself. It was one of the worst nights I ever had. We ended up staying awake the whole night— yelling or crying. He just couldn't understand that I needed to be away for a while. Then the next day he started acting different. He was extremely nice. He said he wanted to please me and work things out, but I don't think we ever can. We just have so many problems that I don't see how they are ever going to get solved. The last time we spoke about my desire to get a separation, Charles said he would do whatever I wanted. Then he said that if I left with Billy, he would kill himself. I don't know if I believe him."

In a relationship between two people, it is unusual for them both to develop, change, and grow in the same ways and at the same pace. Anne has stopped projecting her dream figure onto her husband. By pulling away almost all the aspects of the dream projection from Charles, she has freed herself to move from him and their relationship into new territories. Unfortunately but quite typically, this movement has been into an area of great pain and confusion. Often when people find themselves in a new emotional climate, everything looks different. Psychologists have studied how our present situation has a profound influence on our memories of things past. Many people in a crisis situation such as Anne is experiencing have a tendency to forget the qualities that first attracted them to their lovers. They feel, think, and act as though their relationship had no past. If they do acknowledge that once they loved their partner, this is mentioned in an inarticulate, amorphous fashion, with the quick rejoinder that of course this person is now completely changed. In this regard, Anne is not typical. She can remember and in fact makes a point of talking about the qualities and idiosyncrasies that initially drew her to Charles. Her description of how she liked the smoke surrounding him as he spoke is an eloquent metaphor for that beginning stage of their relationship when she was surrounding him with her animus projection.

But, as Anne tells us, when the comfortable, hazy smoke began to clear, she began to experience the discomfort of confronting the differences between Charles and her dream figure. Realizing that there were serious problems in her relationship, she took a drastic step—she became pregnant. This decision marks the initiation of the strategy she has used throughout to deal with the projection breakdown—avoidance of Charles. She has turned away from him and toward her child. This dramatic movement is followed in all aspects of their relationship. She turns from him and then suffers because of the distance that exists between them. From what she has told us, she seems unwilling to discuss her feelings with Charles, yet she says she is unhappy when he is "unwilling to be involved with my feelings and needs." She is miserable with their sexual relationship but elects to endure it rather than discuss it. In fact, she discusses nothing with Charles. "I certainly haven't been able to tell him about Frank." This pattern of unhappiness, pain, and avoidance marks everything she has told us.

Although Charles was not interviewed, it is quite apparent that he is in at least as much pain as Anne. At about the time that they were expecting their child, he felt that he was no longer special to her. His insecurity was evidently displaced into economic concerns and his anger directed at the medical profession. On some level, he was probably aware that Anne wanted a baby because she no longer wanted him.

Like Anne, Charles seems unwilling to face their problems directly. He continues to have sex with his wife although it must be painfully obvious to him that she does not enjoy it. He is insecure, angry, and jealous and not sure what to do about it. Although he may not say it in these words, he is afraid that among Anne's new friends, she will find someone upon whom to project those qualities she has withdrawn from him. And on this point, his perceptions are correct. He has been told not to be jealous, that he is too possessive and dominating, that Anne "needs more space," when in fact she is in love with another man.

Gregory Bateson, an eminent contemporary philosopher, has suggested that if people are "double-binded"—damned if they do, damned if they don't—they will become sick or go crazy. If a child senses that his father is proud and admiring when he fights and acts aggressively but at the same time yells and punishes him, the child becomes confused. If your partner *acts* cold and distant and *says,* "Don't worry, honey, you know I love you," what should you do? If we live in an atmosphere of lies and double meaning, Bateson found that we can go mad.[4] This is what is happening to Charles. He senses that Anne is unfaithful, but she tells him nothing except that he must give her room and not be so cloying. It is precisely this kind of communication that puts Charles in a double bind. Anne tells us that Charles is emotionally unbalanced and has threatened suicide.

With their breakdown, the dream projections float about with no hook on which to hang. It is difficult to tell which member of the couple is more miserable. Certainly the target from whom the dream image is taken—Charles, in this case—is in for a hard time.

There are a variety of ways in which the target figure reacts when he or she is stripped of the dream projection. There is the kind of reaction Charles has shown; he has answered Anne's rejection with force and anger. It has caused him to place more value on their life together than he had previously. Although before he was confronted with the prospect of separation, he spent little positive energy on developing his relationship with his family, when he is faced with its loss, he reacts violently. He uses strong-arm tactics, confusing Anne by saying she should stay home more or get a full-time job, relating to her largely with anger and impatience, and inducing severe guilt by threatening suicide if she attempts to leave. He is using force in his attempt to hold the projections together, but force will not avail. He is miserable, but he does not help himself or Anne to make the positive changes that would be necessary to salvage their life together.

Other people react to being rejected by reciprocating—by rejecting the partner. When they sense that they are no longer regarded as marvelous, they leave the relationship to look for someone who will again make them feel valued, someone else who will project the dream figure onto them. Often these processes are occurring almost simultaneously, so that it is hard to tell who is leaving whom and why.

Sometimes the target figure does nothing. By remaining motionless, by pretending that everything is as it should be, they attempt to keep the projection upon them. But this will not work. Because while they are standing still, the projection continues to move away.

Anne needs to "own" or become the dream figure she has withdrawn from Charles. This means that she needs to develop in herself many of the qualities she projected upon him at the start of their relationship. She told us that she was drawn to what she saw as his sense of justice, his ability to grasp and articulate ideas. Her return to graduate school may be an attempt to develop these abilities in herself. However, the main strategy she seems to be following is to project her dream figure onto Frank, a mirage she barely knows and rarely sees. This refusal to deal with problems in a direct manner makes the prognosis for her marriage poor. She and Charles have such a long history of nonconfrontation that it may be impossible for them to salvage their relationship or even to find out if it is worth making the attempt to do so.

Many couples like Anne and Charles reach a crucial point in their own development as separate human beings and as partners to one another. The potential risks and gains at this point are high. Which of the number of possible paths we choose will profoundly affect us. Unfortunately not one of them is smooth. To make matters more confusing, often a couple is unaware that they are at a crossroad at all. It is sometimes years before hindsight clearly spots the decision that was made. Sometimes this realization never occurs.

Many of us are not aware of our part in the process of our life choices. Quite the opposite, during this stormy period, we often feel we're not in control of the way we are going. We feel caught up in circumstances, blown by chance. In describing this situation, some respondents have said things like, "The relationship is changing," "Nothing is going right anymore," "Things are out of control." Most often they said, "He (or she) has changed."

Many people tended to see their problems as caused by their partner. They were largely unaware of their own part in the transformation of the relationship from a great romance into something else. This is unfortunate, for we can live to regret decisions made so unconsciously.

The survey indicated that there are various paths couples can take when their relationship reaches this point. Let's look at the most obvious choice, the most extreme turn to take, first—leaving. Although this can often be a dead end for many people, it is a path most well traveled by many American couples today.

The Path of Abandonment: Carl

Carl is twenty-seven. Before his relationship with Joan, he had never been involved in a serious relationship with a woman. "During college, I had a number of girl friends, none of them very long-term. I guess basically I felt superior to them. My interests were broader; I felt intellectually and emotionally more mature. I don't know. Somehow I never took them very seriously and was never surprised or even very disappointed when the relationships began to fizzle. I knew that I would someday find a really together woman, someone very mature, not interested in an overly dependent relationship, someone beyond the limited interests of the people I had dated. Then I got pretty involved in my new job as an assistant editor. I met a lot of new people and began to date some different women. But somehow they seemed either very pretentious or very shallow—very into impressing me with their knowledge of publishing and the big city. I didn't feel comfortable. I felt like it was all a big charade. Things went along like that for a while, and then I met Joan.

"Joan is a teacher. Suddenly everything was right. We felt comfortable together immediately. I thought she was very down to earth—that's the only way to put it—very quiet and real. But very, very smart—she was interested in many of the same things I was. We could really be open with each other, or I thought that we could. I was so relaxed with her, without any of the pretense I had experienced with other women. We were very much in love and spent all our free time together. We decided to live together after a few months. It seemed silly not to. After all, we were always together anyway. I thought Joan would be very easy to live with. She would understand the demands of my job and be supportive of my career, interested in my work. Since she has a somewhat more flexible work schedule than I do, I thought that she could do more of the daily chores, which I usually had little time for. I thought she would feel fine about that.

"Anyway, we lived together for almost two years. To make the story simple: the first year was like I had always imagined it would be. We were dynamite together. I really understood the word *partner* in a new way. Joan understood me perfectly. I could just be myself, and so could she. Well, the first year was great and the second year was awful. I've thought about it a lot and the word that always comes to mind to describe that second year is *betrayal*. I felt fooled. I had put my trust and love in one person and I really began to feel that she had fooled me. I think she understood me so well that she acted the way I wanted her to, and then something happened. Maybe she couldn't keep her act together anymore. She became who she really was. It's so hard to describe—she just wasn't the Joan I knew anymore.

"Things began to go wrong in January. I get low in the winter in the city, with all the cold and slush, and my back usually starts to bother me. Joan always used to be great when I was feeling down. She'd really cheer me up and bring me little gifts, make special meals, things like that. She knew just how to make me feel better. But this time she just didn't. She was occupied with her job, and she didn't have the energy for me. She didn't understand how bad I was feeling. I know it seems trivial, but really for me, that was a turning point. I felt awful. When she did act nice to me, I felt that she was too solicitous, too overbearing. We weren't right anymore. One of the most important things was that I realized she wasn't as honest and warm as I once thought. She also wasn't so smart. And she became cloying. I really felt like an idiot. I had really made a big mistake about her. I felt angry, and we began to argue a lot. Anyway, almost two years from when we moved in together, I had had enough and I left. I moved into a friend's apartment on a temporary basis. Joan was trying to work things out, but I didn't see any point to it. I didn't want to. She didn't understand me at all. When I said that I felt that she had been fooling me, she acted like she didn't know what I was saying. You see, not so smart. I told her that I had waited a long time for a real relationship and I wasn't willing to settle for a charade again. She didn't know what I was saying. Anyway, I'm on my own again and it's not as much fun as I thought it would be. It's going to take time for me to get over this. But I know I will. I had spent so much of my free time with Joan that I've lost contact with a lot of people. I'm also apprehensive about getting really involved with someone else again. But things will get better. I know what I'm looking for."

Carl's experience is typical of many people we interviewed. Although his relationship had many positive aspects working in it, still it failed. Why? Although, as in any phase of any relationship, there were different forms of projection operating and interacting, Carl's projection of the dream girl or anima and the gradual dissolution of this figure strongly dominate the landscape of his story. By the time he had met and fallen in love with Joan, his anima figure was well developed. Like a complete person, it had a whole suite of personality traits—smart, warm, understanding, down to earth, and so on. It is interesting to meet this figure. During the course of the interview, Carl was unknowingly revealing a lot about her.

For a while, the fit between Joan and the anima figure was quite good. Much of the strength of Carl's love for her came out of this congruence. He was seeing in Joan the reflection of the anima whom he had sought before but never found. Since there were many places where reality and the projected figure were close, Joan was able to hold the projection well. However, this state of affairs could not go on forever. For Carl, one chink in the armor, one space where a part of Joan that was not a part of the dream girl showed through, and he had to leave. He could not face the fact that he was having a relationship with a woman and not a perfect goddess. Because all the anima qualities remained externalized, unrecognized, and unowned, he could only see Joan as the source of his "betrayal." He could see only one path open to him—leaving. His lack of awareness of the processes involved blinded him to alternate routes. By leaving, he may have lost the possibility of learning more about Joan and also about himself. By turning his back on the relationship, he turned his back on this kind of understanding. It is likely that he will bring the burden of his relationship with Joan—along with all the unresolved conflicts—to his next relationship.

It is certainly possible that he will work through these problems on his own. He told us that he plans to travel, and this may give him the opportunity for some needed self-reflection. But the dialogue of a relationship is a much better forum for working out projections than the monologue of self-reflection. Some people we interviewed were unable to deal with their projections in early relationships because either they or their partner were too immature. They ended these relationships but were able to reach an understanding of their projections in later ones. Leaving is not always inappropriate. Carl may be able to accomplish by himself or with someone else what he was unable to work through with Joan.

Joan began to seem "cloying" to Carl. It is interesting that the feeling of being smothered or confined by one's partner is a common one for the withdrawing person to experience. Actually she or he is feeling suffocated by all the projections of ideal qualities which once were tightly tied onto the partner. Now as these projections begin to fall off, the person feels buried under them.

For many people today, this pattern is repeated. After leaving one relationship when dream-figure projections break down, people seek them again in someone else. "Serial monogamy" is simply this—going from one relationship to another, falling in love, becoming disillusioned, and then casting off the burden of a real relationship in favor of a liaison with a dream figure. The statistics on divorce confirm our finding that many people fall into this pattern. A remarkably high percentage of people who are divorced have been so before.[5]

Each time this path is chosen again, it becomes more and more difficult to choose a different route. The burden of the ideal figure becomes heavier and heavier. Unfortunately, by abandoning each relationship as the gap between fantasy and reality becomes obvious, people also abandon the opportunity to get to know the dream figure. By choosing to repeat this pattern, the anima/animus becomes hidden further and further in the darkness of our unconscious. This darkness obscures our relationships more and more totally. What this means is that it becomes increasingly difficult for us to establish a clear relationship with another.

Many of the people interviewed said they feel frustrated and trapped in this pattern. Gradually and more acutely they feel that each new relationship is lacking in depth, intensity, possibility. Each one is exciting for an ever-decreasing period of time. People often express the feeling that they themselves are lacking, that they are unable to sustain and nurture a meaningful relationship. They feel less in control of their lives and more and more the victim of some malady for which they know no cure.

The Path of Denial: Dana

For many people, the fear of being alone is paralyzing. They blind themselves to much that is unpleasant and disturbing, endure much that is uncomfortable or even painful in order to sustain a relationship. Many people equate exploring the feelings and dynamics of their projections with confrontation and pain. They are fatalistic and resigned when it comes to their lives. They feel that they are incapable of changing them. Living with the familiar, however unsatisfying it is, is often chosen over venturing into unknown territory. There is comfort in the known, fear in the unknown. Often they refuse to confront anything connected to the projection breakdown that might threaten their lives as they have arranged them.

Dana, a woman of twenty-eight, gave us the following account of her marriage. "I know that things will never change for Walter and me. I can see us in twenty years being just as we are today. We got married young. I was twenty and he was twenty-one. We have both always worked all the time, and four years ago, we bought our house. It is what we have always dreamed of, and now finally it is ours. Things between us are in a pattern; they never change. Our lives are on a schedule. Walter doesn't like to delve too much into our relationship. I agree with him. He thinks it is pointless and self-indulgent. I don't like fighting. My parents fought a lot, and I always vowed I'd never be in that kind of relationship. We both like things quiet. What's the point of shouting and getting upset? We have things pretty well worked out between us. I guess you could call us both pretty private people. We respect that in each other. It makes us well suited and good companions. Maybe it would be better if one of us were a little more outgoing, but I don't think so.

"I can't really think of a current problem. One problem we almost had was about two years ago, when I began to think about having a child. My first cousin had just had a baby, and he was really cute. Our house is big enough, and we have a yard. I thought it might be the right time. We had never really talked about it at length before. I brought the subject up, and we discussed it. Walter is very good about discussions. Whenever we decide to talk about something, he really gives the topic his full attention and is very calm and rational. It makes me feel good to know that there won't be scenes and we'll really accomplish what we set out to do. He's really quite good at looking at a problem clearly; he's very reasonable. Anyway, Walter pointed out that we had finally gotten our house, something we both had worked very hard for, and that to have a baby would be a real financial burden. He showed me that many things that we both enjoy doing would have to be sacrificed. Both of us take classes at night at the community college, and these would have to go.

"He asked if I was unhappy or felt a lack in my life and I had to say no. I saw that a baby would be more of a disruption than an addition, and being jealous of my cousin—Walter said that that was what it was—wasn't a good reason to bring a child into the world. Really his arguments were very sound and straight. I realized I wasn't that clear in my own reasoning. So we dropped the idea. For a while, I felt kind of depressed and disappointed. I felt that I wanted to be clearer about my own feelings, and that I hadn't expressed my side well. I feel that sometimes, and this bothers me. But this isn't really a problem, because Walter is better at expressing things than I am and most times I agree with him. Anyway it's not a problem between us but my own lack. Now we are working on a greenhouse for the house. Sometimes I feel bad about not being very excited about things, but then I realize that you can't change human nature. We have a good life together. We have our house. We do things together and are content with each other. I'm happy and I am very lucky. I'm sorry I can't think of any more problems to tell you about."

As Dana talked about her relationship, her delivery was flat and her emotional tone even. So, too, in her responses to the questionnaire—everything was normal, fine, no problems, no conflicts, things running on a even keel. Dana, like a great number of people who answered our questionnaire, is happy, satisfied with her life, and very happy in her relationship. How curious it is that although one out of two marriages ends in rupture and divorce, we found so many people with no real problems or conflicts.

Right beneath the surface of Dana's story, however, there is another description of the way things are. As we all know, there are numerous conflicts that arise within a relationship. As the dream projections begin to break down, a tremendous amount of energy circulates within each person and within the relationship. Although Dana didn't discuss what first attracted her to Walter, from her answers to the questionnaire and interview, we can reconstruct a picture of this dream-boy figure with whom she fell in love. He was always calm, in control, strong, and rational. He was also open, warm, accepting, and fair. Dana sees her husband as this person, and she continues to work at keeping this image intact. In order to do this, Walter must cooperate. He too must work at holding the pictures that Dana is projecting onto him. In order to maintain the projections, they both must ignore many aspects of themselves and each other. The breakdown of the projection has occurred. Dana has told us, perhaps unintentionally, that although Walter is acceptable, he is hardly a prince or dream boy. And yet they both defend themselves against this realization. They deny and repress.

Within limits, there are real advantages to being defensive and keeping our eyes closed to the unpleasant. If you are at a family gathering and a relative you dislike is there, there is no point in starting an argument and thinking about how much you dislike that person. At times, it is better for all concerned to look the other way. In every relationship, it is not only uncomfortable, it is impossible constantly to confront every single problem that may arise. Defenses serve a valuable function. In our primary relationships, we require a certain amount of tranquillity and peace. In our families, we desire refuge from a difficult world. Therefore, it

is important that couples do not always grapple with and confront problems and uncomfortable feelings. Learning about ourselves and the other is a very gradual and constant process. We
build on it slowly, and sometimes we need to rest.

There comes a point, however, where the almost complete denial
of problems becomes maladaptive. One of Freud's major contributions was to show that if we ignore or repress too much, we become psychologically impaired or neurotic. As feelings struggle to
emerge and express themselves, another part forces those feelings
out of our awareness. This internal struggle requires much energy
and effort. If our energies are depleted in inner war, we will have
less energy for productive tasks and we will feel anxious and depressed. Ignoring feelings and thoughts is hard work. When our
resources are spent working at denial, we feel exhausted.

When denial or repression operates in the context of a couple or
a group relationship, the partners must cooperate to keep it going.
This cooperation or collusion requires a pact, a silent agreement
to avoid confronting the unpleasant, the conflicts, the inevitable
changes. The pact is an unconscious or only partly conscious one.
Its rules and by-laws are complex, and often we are unaware of
them. Its basic purpose is to allow both members of the couple to
deny the threat of change, the existence of discordant feelings and
thoughts that arise as projections break down.

Walter and Dana are in collusion about almost all aspects of
their relationship. It is no wonder that Dana's emotional tone is
flat. She and her husband have concentrated their energies on
maintaining the surface calm of their lives, and it takes much energy to sustain the status quo. Let's examine the details of their
agreement, for while there are benefits to the contract, there are
also limits. While it frees them from the anxiety of the unknown,
it also constrains them. In order to live up to each other's projections, they can only act in certain ways. To move too far out of the
limits is to break down the whole structure. The notion of
projection is based upon the connection between projector and
target. To move away from this mutual system in one area means
that the entire structure is endangered.

Dana and Walter have agreed that conflict should be avoided at
all cost. They want to maintain the emotional tone of their life together. They are terrified of upsetting the apple cart. So they
maintain a daily pattern of activity. Things must go on as usual.
Keeping things running on schedule makes it easier to exclude
any intrusions that might disrupt their lives.

We can see that their style of solving problems also serves to keep away any potential threat, any negative feeling they might have about each other. Stating arguments cogently and clearly has become their primary goal in dealing with their problems (which they deny they have). They have agreed that if an opinion cannot be stated quickly or clearly, it should not be included. Dana and Walter have adopted this strategy so that they will not probe too deeply into their emotions. Often our most important feelings aren't easily verbalized, but to ignore them because they are difficult to put into words is a serious mistake. Another aspect of their collusion is that they have adopted Walter's style of solving their nonexistent problems and, further, they have agreed that he is better at it.

Dana imagines that her husband is fair and reasonable, yet it seems that he bullied her out of wanting a child though they both denied that he did so. Dana goes so far as to say that this was "almost" a problem, but not quite. If she opened her eyes to the fact that to some extent Walter is not so wonderful, that he is not so fair, they would both have to confront the broken projections and the people behind them. They do not do this, and they pay a high price for their emotional calm.

Dana's depression and dissatisfaction, which she quickly disavows, are nonetheless evident. Not only their style of problem solving but the roles they play have become rigid or frozen. They both cling tightly to their images—the ones they project and the ones they hold. By struggling to hold onto their projections, they have frozen all the energy in which these projections partake. In denying that any conflict exists in the relationship, they deny the existence of two multidimensional and complete people. Ideal men and women, the dream images, do not battle—they are eternally compatible—and that is the illusion this couple is struggling to perpetuate.

What happens when people spend so much energy keeping their eyes closed to the projection breakdown? Well, for one thing, they may never wake up. A man and woman may become completely frozen in their fairy tale, insisting that the other be the stereotype of his or her sex. If a man does not develop and become conscious of his own dream girl and if a woman does not develop her dream boy, they will have formed a symbiotic relationship with not even the vitality of one person.

Many older couples who responded to the questionnaire who had been together for twenty or more years said that they were happy and that there were no problems in their relationship.

However, they complained of boredom and expressed the desire for increased sharing and affection. Dana says she can see herself in twenty years being just as she is now. What a depressing prospect. Can safety be worth such imprisonment?

Before leaving the discussion of the path of denial, one more point should be made. When a couple freezes their projections, they may be inviting very serious trouble. The frozen structure built by years of denial may eventually break down under the weight of a problem. When this happens, the couple often discovers that they have not acquired the skills necessary to deal with conflict. Not only have they neglected to learn the skills, but they have neglected to learn about themselves and each other. They feel confronted by mystery. But there is a way out of the mystery.

Owning the Anima/Animus: Edward

When we project the dream boy or girl onto our partner, we are living in a dream world. The breakdown of the projection, however discomforting, signifies that we may be able to wake up from this dream and actually get to know our partner as another real person. We can do this by withdrawing our projection and becoming what we project.

In order to become or "own" the projection, we must first identify it. What is this dream boy or girl really like? When the projection breaks down, it is sometimes very difficult to enumerate the qualities of the dream image because they don't fit neatly onto one single target. But you can start to do it if you imagine the person you love, or used to love, or someone you know or want very much to know.

This man or woman you long for—what is he or she like? Exactly what is it about this person that captivates and possesses you? Is your dream girl caring, warm, emotional, sensitive, artistic, intuitive, mysterious? Does your dream boy know the answers to your most perplexing questions? Is he strong, adventurous, protective, kind, powerful? If you try to become as specific as possible about the qualities that impress, influence, and fascinate you, you can begin to identify many apsects of the anima or animus. Our dreams can help us here. Occasionally we find in them an incredible person, a romantic figure who is totally mesmerizing. Often this star of our dreams is our anima/animus figure. By thinking about what makes this person so desirable, we can learn about the qualities of our dream figure.

It is possible to become conscious of the dream boy or girl by examining and trying to become the qualities we project onto our lovers. Instead of demanding that your partner be those parts of your personality you have neglected to develop, you can take the responsibility and develop those facets in yourself. You can take back within yourself just those qualities you sought in your partner.

As both members of the couple become their projections, their relationship becomes one between two relatively whole and independent people rather than a symbiotic union of two incomplete halves projecting their own unknown faces. As long as the couple projects, the union can hardly be called a relationship, since both members are in a sense asleep and dreaming each other. To truly relate to another person, we must be awake.

The key to solving the problem brought about by the breakdown of our dream projections seems to lie in the ability of couples to share the responsibility for feelings and events no matter how unpleasant these might be. They do not blame their partner for not being what they themselves have been unable to become. Thus becoming or owning our projections involves the very difficult work of developing one's own potential in conjunction with another. What ideally is happening is a parallel growth wherein each partner is helped and nourished by the development of the other. Our respondents who reported this kind of progress—who were able to evolve successful solutions to conflicts—made it clear to us that there are no quick, easy, or foolproof methods. This can be seen in the following case.

Edward is in his late forties. He and Jennifer have four children and live in a large house in the suburbs of a metropolitan area. "My career was moving ahead as it should have. The contacts I made at Harvard helped me get established with an excellent petroleum corporation. It seemed that everything I touched—production, refining, marketing, whatever—resulted in an excellent return on investment. The reviews I received from my managers were uniformly outstanding. I worked hard, exercised good judgment, was creative, and I believe I brought out the best in the people I managed. By the time I was forty, I oversaw retail operations for a large section of the country, and over a thousand people fell under my purview.

"For the first twelve years of our marriage, there were few problems or conflicts. I was happy with my career, not so much because of the money, though there was enough, to be sure, but because I liked getting things done and being in a position of power. Jennifer was great with the children and was also very involved with local cultural groups. We enjoyed our dinners together and occasional weekend trips. I have always had a passion for fast cars and was able to buy myself a Ferrari.

"I look back on that period of my life as being very harmonious. I felt that everything clicked and was moving along right on course. But then things started to come apart. One weekend we went up to a new country home our friends had just bought. We have known this couple for almost twenty years—since college. I consider David to be my best friend—at least, I used to. I remember that I was looking forward to the weekend quite a bit, but it turned into a very uncomfortable time for me. I felt very left out. Jennifer spent a great deal of time talking with both David and Lynne. They all seemed very close. But when I spoke to either of them, the conversation quickly became chitchat. All of a sudden, it dawned on me that this was the extent of my interactions with all my friends. Jennifer had real friends, while I had acquaintances—acquaintances I had known for twenty years! I felt jealous and then I felt really depressed. After that, I started feeling restless and more and more dissatisfied.

"I can honestly say that before that, I had never felt that kind of deep unhappiness. After so many years of being faithful to Jenny, my head began to turn. At first, these affairs were very brief. But my relationship with one woman became more serious and our meetings became more frequent. I suppose this is what you would refer to as my mid-life crisis; it was hell. I was in a pressure cooker at work. I had always relished the responsibility and authority, but now all I was feeling were the pressures of the accountability. My home life was rapidly deteriorating. I yelled a lot; I just had no patience. I couldn't talk to the children at all. And the woman whom I was seeing wanted me to "make a commitment," to leave Jen and marry her.

"Well, I knew I didn't want that, but I didn't know what I wanted. By this time, Jenny and two of the kids were at the beach house. Usually I come up on the weekend. This time I didn't. The first couple of weekends, I made excuses that involved work. This wasn't unusual. I had legitimately had to do this before. The third weekend in a row that I called to tell Jen I couldn't make it, she sounded pretty upset. But I couldn't deal with it. I was too involved with myself and my problems and I blustered my way through. In the middle of the next week, she called and said that

she didn't want to hear any more excuses. She insisted that I come
up or she was coming down to the city. You've got to know Jenny
to know this was unusual. I knew right away that something was
going to happen.

"So I guess it was Jenny's decision, not mine, to face the music.
She really forced me into it. That weekend I went up to the house,
and we began to talk. Things just came out. I was very frazzled
and I wasn't very coherent. I told Jen about my lady friend. I told
her about work. I told her it was awful. I talked and talked. She
was very upset, but I couldn't comfort or even listen to her. I was
caught up in my own feelings and problems. Nothing was resolved
or anything, except that we both decided that I shouldn't come up
for a few weeks. I guess we both wanted some time off. This whole
time was painful. The summer was awful. I went up a few times
but things were pretty bad, even into the fall. We really tried to
talk, but it was very difficult. But gradually and slowly, things
began to come together a little. Jen and I spent a lot of time talking about ourselves—who we were and what we were doing. We
spoke about my work, and Jen made some suggestions about how I
could try to be a little less obsessed with it. I broke off my affair
and sort of felt a little foolish about the whole thing. It's hard to
put together now, but I would sum it up by saying that for the
first time, I spent a lot of time talking about my life instead of
just going ahead and doing business as usual.

"About two years ago, I left the company and started my own
consulting firm. So far it's been a joy. I still like the challenge, but
I have more flexible time. I've tried to change the pattern of work
first; family, friends, and everything else later. I've even taken an
evening class in pottery with Jen. I love it. I'm really surprised at
how relaxing I find it."

Edward's story is one of personal development that emphasizes
fairly exclusively a one-sided growth. His career success was
achieved at the expense of whole other aspects of his personality—his "feeling side" or emotional life. In order for him to do as
well as he did, he pursued a definite direction, with few stops or
side trips. Because so much of his energy and attention were consumed in his career and because the fit between Jennifer and his
anima was a good one, a long period of time elapsed before the
breakdown of the dream projection and its attendant crises occurred.

Although a long period of time had gone by with his situation remaining stable, internal pressures finally caused the structure to topple. The anima is very much engaged with emotions and feeling connections to others. Edward had almost totally neglected this side of himself, putting the full burden of his emotional life upon his wife. She was the one who was involved with their children and friends, for example. Edward thus felt freed of emotional responsibility. However, because he was unaware of his emotional life and projected it onto his wife, that did not mean that it ceased to exist. Eventually it moved into consciousness, bringing restlessness and discontent. No matter how quickly he attempted to outrun it, his feelings caught up with him. Even the fastest Ferrari was no match for his unconscious. When his anima burst forth into his awareness, its weight broke down his projection onto Jennifer. His feelings could not be contained easily within himself and they could not fit neatly onto his wife. Edward tried projecting them onto a number of other targets. His dream-girl image even settled for a while on one particular other woman.

Very often, the serious conflicts that couples report tend to be symptomatic of their one-sided development. In a society where division of labor and specialization are most valued, it is almost impossible not to develop unevenly. To be successful in business, the arts, sports, or just about any career including parenting, we must look straight ahead and march forward, brushing aside all distractions, even if these distractions are our own feelings or thoughts. We deposit these "distractions" on our mates in the dream-boy or -girl projection and push ahead.

We are more complex than this kind of development allows room for. Like Edward, we may attempt to brush aside those parts of ourselves that are "interfering" with the task at hand, with the movement of our lives as we have tried to define them. But often, we cannot do this indefinitely. The anima and animus are symbols for basic areas of our beings. Those neglected aspects often strongly press upon us for their fulfillment. As Edward has shown us, their demands often begin to make themselves felt as dissatisfactions, which rapidly build to major unhappiness the longer we attempt to ignore them.

Many people interpret the dissatisfaction they feel with their lives at such a juncture as a justification for condemning and rejecting those aspects of themselves they have spent years developing. It is most unfortunate to see case after case of people who reach the point of recognizing their one-sided development only to turn around and reject what they have accomplished in order to "work on" other parts of themselves. It is as though they recognize that they have jumped off one side of the boat, so they climb back on board to jump off the other. In this way, the same destructive pattern is perpetuated. There is development of only one aspect of the personality at the expense of the other. One man was interviewed who had been a fairly successful lawyer. He quit his job and left his family and home to become a musician. For him, becoming aware of the anima meant giving everything else up. But becoming conscious of the projected dream figure does not always necessitate rejection of the rest of the personality. It means augmenting it.

Our survey has uncovered a number of cases of women whose stories seem to be mirror images of Edward's; that is, they have reversed the emphasis of their development. Their early adulthood was focused on the evolution of their "feeling function," their emotional lives. This emphasis is expressed in the development of intimate bonds with friends and family. In this pattern, the projected animus contains the opposite "thinking function." When their dream-boy projection breaks down—when their mates no longer satisfactorily can contain its weight—they often work on its development by devoting their energies to professional and career interests. This appropriate and constructive move, however, is sometimes accompanied by an equally inappropriate and destructive one. While they were embracing a career, some women who were interviewed rejected their emotional ties, particularly with their families. They felt a great deal of anger at the fact that they had neglected so much of their own development. This anger seemed to blind them to the fact that they had not been standing still at all. They had been growing, but only in certain aspects of themselves. Blame was placed upon the family for "stunting" their growth. This particular pattern is typical of our society, which places little value on the development of the feeling functions. Somehow this kind of growth—which is surely just as complex and difficult as that of the "thinking functions"—is regarded as inferior. So people (and these people tended to be women) who have devoted their energies to this side of themselves felt their incompleteness quite acutely.

Edward proceeded in a way that enabled him to build on what he had achieved. Because he needed to grow emotionally did not mean that he had to discard his intellect. Because his relationship with Jennifer was unsatisfying didn't mean he had to discard it.

He didn't drop out. Instead, he transformed his job, his relationship, and himself. All these were altered as he incorporated more of the dream girl into his being.

Incorporating rather than rejecting may seem initially to be very difficult. As this new side is allowed to grow, we are inexperienced in dealing with it. Our more developed parts may overwhelm our newly emerging one. We may at first feel as if we are involved in an exceedingly complex and tricky balancing act. Like Edward, many people experience a period of intense confusion and disorientation. Looking at things with a new perspective can certainly be a dizzying experience. It's common for both men and women to have a strong desire for time alone—the quiet to sort things out and get to know themselves again. They seem to be asking for the opportunity to find equilibrium again. When people have allowed this process to continue, they have found that these two sides augment, enrich, and balance each other rather than only competing for energy.

Owning our opposite means even more than a change in attitude; it means we must take the actions necessary to become what we have projected onto others, to develop those aspects of ourselves that are unsophisticated and undifferentiated. Edward made major changes in his life in order to incorporate the dream girl into himself. He gave up his job and started a new one; he began taking classes and spent more time with his family. As he came to own his dream-girl figure, he became more sensitive and warm. In fact, he speaks about his new business with the feeling of a parent nurturing a baby. He specifically told us at the end of the interview that he was taking pottery lessons. This is an indication that he is giving an education to his feelings.

Effective Communication

In Chapter 3, we discussed the notion that a couple or a family is a system. There cannot be change in one part of the system without corresponding changes in the other parts. Edward did not give much detail about Jennifer, but it seems quite clear that she is an emotionally complex, intelligent, and mature woman who was willing to change. Like many other people, she experienced the breakdown of her partner's dream projection with distress. Jennifer had been content in the relationship and then suddenly found herself no longer prized. She had to confront the fact that Edward had been involved with another woman.

We have seen in this chapter that force and anger, rejection
and denial are all ways in which people have reacted when their
partner's projections have broken down. Jennifer used none of
these. She apparently had an adequate sense of her own identity
apart from Edward's projection. When his projections dissolved,
she did not fall apart. Had she done so, she might have forced Edward's projections underground, thereby rupturing or stagnating
the relationship. Instead, she was willing to accept change in her
partner and to change herself. She was supportive of Edward and
able to communicate effectively to him. Edward's success in owning his anima had much to do with Jennifer.

Generally if an individual is attempting to own his dream projections, the cooperation of the partner is essential.

Receiving the projections of another is dangerous business. In
Chapters 7 and 8 we shall see how entertainers and politicians can
thrive or sometimes die because of the projections of their fans.
When we receive the projection of the dream boy or girl, we are
taking credit for qualities we do not deserve. When these projections break down, we pay the piper because we are blamed. As
couples described their dissatisfactions, troubles, and conflicts
concerning possessiveness, jealousy, insufficient sharing, and lack
of communication, they often saw their partner as being the cause
of their troubles. Blame is the dominant theme of the projection
breakdown.

If the attempt to solve conflict begins with the attitude that
everything that is wrong is the fault of the partner, the couple
will naturally be unable to find constructive solutions. If the communication process begins with blame, the partner feels attacked,
and rightly so. They become threatened and defensive. In this
way, blaming your partner for what is bothering you is the surest
way to close down the communication and begin a fight.

When we feel blamed or attacked, we become dishonest. We
know that if we reveal vulnerability at some point, our partner
will seize upon it and use it against us in the battle. When blame
is a central feature of the dialogue, even honesty serves to perpetuate the battle. Honesty can be used not to further communication but as a weapon in the battle of blame. When couples described their styles of communication during conflicts, it was clear
that some people used brute force in the name of honesty. If your
partner is sensitive about some physical or personality characteristic, honest communication does not mean calling attention to the
fact that you do not like that particular quality. Nor does honesty

necessarily mean dredging up every unpleasant thought or feeling you ever had about your life together. This kind of "honest communication" only perpetuates the fight. If we are interested in developing honest communication, a gradual opening up seems to be required rather than an assault.

We saw that Edward and Jennifer were able to speak honestly to each other and to sort out projection from reality. They not only had the ability to talk about even their most difficult and threatening feelings, they had the courage to do so. This courage is probably the single most crucial reason why their relationship has survived and grown.

To understand the workings of the projection process is to realize that the dissatisfactions emanating from the dream projection cannot strictly be the fault of one partner. While they surely may be lacking in one or a number of ways, our own unhappiness cannot be blamed totally on their deficiencies. Rather it is due to our own incomplete development.

When we experience a need to grow, it feels like any other unfulfilled need such as hunger, thirst, sex; as painful or as frustrating. When we recognize our responsibility, the part we play in our problems, the most appropriate way to begin the dialogue may be to ask for help rather than to blame.

The task of becoming what we project is not easy, and we need all the help we can get. The people we interviewed who were happiest in their relationships seemed to be able to help their partners and be helped by them. They were not overwhelmingly threatened by change and were able to take sensible risks. This means that to some extent, they were able to talk about feelings and aspects of themselves that were not easy to reveal—their feelings of attraction for others, of jealousy, or fear of being alone, for instance. For these couples, the feelings of disappointment and disenchantment that came with the projection breakdown brought with them the opportunity to open wider areas of communication and self-understanding.

6

On the Job

"As a nurse, I have always gone by the rule, Never treat a patient or his family any different, *no matter what,* than you would want yourself or your family treated. So this is what I do. I'm careful to follow this rule. I consider myself very professional in my approach to my job."

Many of the people who spoke about their work were very serious about their jobs and expressed a similar commitment to "professionalism." Although they wanted to do their work conscientiously, they complained that other people were obstacles to this goal. Their co-workers distracted them, annoyed them, deflected their energies from the tasks at hand.

"I love my work. I find reporting and writing exciting, challenging, meaningful. But I find I'm not allowed to do it. It's office politics—you get drawn in whether you want to or not. My fantasy is that I could have an office that was completely separate from everyone else's where I could work in peace. My only contact with everyone would be through machines."

This theme—people as obstacles—kept coming up time and again in conversations, both formal and informal, about work. And we also found that these obstacles were not the other people at all but rather our projections onto them.

Why should projection be so prevalent on the job? What is it *in particular* about most job settings that makes them breeding grounds for projection? There are two factors: the necessity to deny and repress our emotions at work, and the fact that at work, we take on a particular role.

Although personal feelings, subjectivity, and favoritism are not supposed to have a place in our business life, they do. No matter how firm our intention to go in, get our work done, collect our paycheck, and leave, most people find that the tasks outlined in the job description are only a small part of what they are expected to do, who they are at work, and how people relate to them.

On the job, you both know and do not know the people around you. They are your intimates in terms of time, and in most cases, you are dependent upon them to fulfill their job obligations so that you can fulfill yours. Although we are thrust into this situation of intimacy and dependency, work demands that we pretend we do not have strong feelings about those around us.

Expression of emotion about co-workers is not sanctioned, but our feelings do not dissolve just because work is not considered the proper arena for their expression. If your boss doesn't acknowledge your contributions and keeps passing you up for a promotion, you are definitely not supposed to cry or pull the door off the hinges. Rather you should arrange a meeting in which you tactfully express your concerns. If one of your colleagues is not competent and therefore burdens you, you should not scream or kick but perhaps have a talk in which you casually insert a few suggestions on how you can more efficiently work together. If you develop a big crush on the new guy or girl down the hall, smiling pleasantly and making mild inquiries about how he or she is getting along are all that's appropriate.

The demand to deny intimate feelings in this public setting gives rise to tension. The internal pressure of denied emotions and the external pressure of the demand to perform causes people to misperceive, to misinterpret, and to project.

On the job, we all assume a role. Roles facilitate the denial of emotions, dictating what we can and cannot feel. A *role* is defined as "prescribed actions and words." It is a sociological term derived from the theater. If one takes on a role in a play, one must act and speak certain lines. There is some flexibility—the role can be interpreted in many ways—but dialogue cannot be invented; there are restrictions. On the job, we gradually shape ourselves to fit the role.

When we assume a role on the job, we not only are likely to externalize our inner conflicts and see them in the people around us, we are also very likely to be projected upon. A role is a ready-made target. Many times people talked about the discomfort of being at work, the artificiality of it. This uneasiness often comes from an awareness of the difference between "ourselves" and the way others are seeing us—their projections.

The more "professional" we become, that is, the more rigidly we strive to adhere to our roles, the more likely we are to defeat the purpose of clear detachment for which we long. This is because we must attempt to divorce ourselves from the emotions and impulses that are part of us. It stands to reason, then, that there is just that much more unresolved energy that must go somewhere. Much of it comes out in our projections. The decision we make to exclude our feelings from the business at hand backfires. Although we may feel that we have eliminated subjectivity from our working relationship with others, it surfaces anyway. In fact, we have simply guaranteed that we will be as subjective as possible. What we see in those around us is completely subjective; we see ourselves.

We interviewed people from many different kinds of employment settings. We also made every effort to speak to at least three people at each place we studied. An initial review of notes and interview tapes quickly showed that the differences were far outweighed by the similarities. We decided to pick a medium-sized pharmaceutical firm we will call Redex as a good example of what we found out about projection on the job.

Redex is a successful, moderate-sized company located on the outskirts of a large metropolitan area. It occupies modern, sprawling facilities and employs about a thousand people. The people who work there are either scientists and technicians, who are part of the research facility, or people who are part of the sales division, the technical writing department, the general accounting and business division, and the administration and support staff.

The typical work setup looks in many ways like a family, and Redex is no exception. The family pattern of work organization has been recognized from paternalistic Victorian work situations to the current Japanese "Z" management strategies. The external form of Redex mimics the family, with a strong president (father) and employees (children) organized in sibling systems. But not only does the external form of the organization mimic the family, so also do the internal relationships and the projections that occur. When people find themselves in a family situation, two types of projection come into play—parallel and unconscious. The hierarchy and roles supply the suitable hooks; our repressed emotion provides the material to project upon those hooks.

The Father

Everyone interviewed at Redex, no matter what position he or she held there, spoke at one point or another about "Charles" or "Mr. Hagarth." The most common target for the projection of people on the job is the boss. In almost all situations, from professional to blue collar, there is someone in authority.

Charles Hagarth is the president of Redex, and he really looks the part. A tall, blond New Englander, he roams the halls in blue pinstripes. Charles is cast in the role of the traditional patriarch—distant from the family, dignified, fair and even-handed in his treatment of the "children." Our interview with Charles was quite different from the interviews with other people in the company. What started as an interview quickly became a tour of the company, a list of its accomplishments, and a company "bio" of Charles. He maintained his image and his distance. We found ourselves impressed without wanting to be, as we sat in his huge carpeted office with a full glass wall and tasteful paintings.

The boss is usually at a distance both physical and social from his subordinates. That big office down the hall with the large desk is like the inner throne room of the king. Physical distancing facilitates the kind of separation necessary for the projection of the father to flourish. If he were more accessible, more visible, the projections would be held up more quickly to the light in which they could dissolve.

The success that a good manager enjoys depends in large part upon how good a target he is for the father projection of his subordinates. It is for this reason that younger men and women of any age have trouble being managers. Regardless of the skills they possess, many people have a hard time seeing them as the authority. Power comes from interaction, from the perception of authority, and does not reside solely in the authority figure. If I am unable to see you as an authority, that is, if you are an unsuitable target, one or both of us is in trouble.

A very popular book on executive skills advises that the head of an office ". . . has to address himself to what is important to people from their point of view as well as his own and make sure he doesn't confuse the two. He has to develop the skill of helping people to feel secure, to learn from their own experience, to reach their own decisions, and to become more mature and independent."[1] This sounds very much like advice on good parenting.

Many of our old feelings about our parents lie dormant under our adult personalities, waiting for the requisite stimulus to awaken them. If we have been able in the past to work out our relationship to our parents, we are in a much better position to see, understand, and interact clearly with our bosses. If our feelings about our parents remain unclear, this clouded relationship is transferred to our dealings with a superior who stands in a pseudoparental relationship to us. There is inevitable misunderstanding whenever we deal with the "authority figure." We are tied to our projections, and their weight hinders both our career and personal development.

When we find ourselves in this situation that so duplicates the family, we can take on the role and style we developed in our family of origin. However, we are unaware that we are transferring those feelings onto those around us. We are projecting the contents of our personal unconscious.

The Obedient Child

Robert does basic research for Redex. He graduated with a Ph.D. in biochemistry. A soft-spoken, articulate man in his mid-thirties, he still has the look of a dedicated graduate student. When we asked him how he got along with Charles Hagarth, he told us the following story:

"I was due to go to a conference for three days in San Francisco and had to cancel my meetings for Friday in order to get to the airport on time. Having forgotten the final copy of the paper I was supposed to deliver, I made a last-minute trip to the office to pick it up. On my way out I happened to meet Charles, whom I barely knew, in the elevator. You have to understand that the way things are set up at Redex, the Research Division really has very little to do with the top management. On a day-to-day basis, we are fairly autonomous. Although, of course, I know we are tied to them and their decisions, we don't come into personal contact very often except for company parties, conferences, and the like. So, you see, I'd spoken very little with Charles during my three and a half years there.

"I was immediately seized with overwhelming anxiety. When he said good afternoon to me, I was sure he was being sarcastic about how late it was that I was getting to work. I was sure he looked disapprovingly and suspiciously at me. Even though I know now that he hadn't the slightest idea about my schedule, I was feeling that he knew I had canceled my meetings and regular work for the day. I felt exactly like a kid caught cutting class. It was only after I got on the plane and calmed down that I realized that none of this could possibly have been true. But what is strange is that still when I see him, I always get the feeling that he knows just what's going on and is keeping tabs on me."

Robert was essentially reliving a childhood experience. He felt that his boss was able to read his mind, to know more about him than he himself knew. He projected the cause of his guilt onto Charles and saw him as an omniscient father, while he played the part of the obedient child.

In many work situations, the bosses are not at all involved in our daily activities. They may hardly know our names or what we do, yet if we pass them in the hall, instead of feeling invisible through anonymity, we feel somewhat vulnerable and exposed.

Many people have a great deal of difficulty seeing their parents as other human beings with weaknesses and strengths of their own. They are seen still as the superhuman, all-knowing figures from childhood. People sometimes believe that they aren't really in control, that they can't change the direction of their careers unless their boss changes. They feel he is not only in control of the fate of the office but of their own fate as well.

When this kind of projection occurs, the expectations about the competence, ability, and knowledge of the boss are very high. He is endowed with powers that are unrealistically great. This doesn't mean that those people don't gossip about or even denigrate the boss. But being called to his office, for instance, still evokes tension, nervousness, even fear. The strength of the emotion they attach to him is a clear indication that what they see is not a person but the image of their own projection of authority. When the boss is out of the office, the general atmosphere is relaxed. The father is gone and the children can have a holiday. When he is there, even if he is very removed from their own sphere, they feel that he somehow knows what is going on and exactly how well they are performing their jobs.

The Rebellious Child

For many people, the person in charge is never the object of respect or awe at all. The boss is identified from the beginning as the enemy, the exploiter, the one to be on guard against at all times. People who feel this way are always full of criticism, anger, and resentment. Many are still locked in an unresolved conflict with their parents. This conflict is easily triggered in a work situation in which we must listen to and be evaluated by a person in authority. The authority figure is not seen as who he or she is but rather as the parent from whom disengagement has not occurred.

Laurie was a middle-level manager with the Sales and Promotion Department at Redex and from all reports was quite successful at her job. In fact, she had increasingly taken over much of her boss's work load, doing many of the client presentations and extensive traveling. She was well liked by clients and co-workers alike. However, she didn't feel that her boss, Philip, adequately recognized and appreciated her competence, dedication, and ability. Laurie saw his agreement to allow her to expand her scope of responsibility as motivated by his own laziness rather than by belief in her abilities. Although he often praised her, it was in the joking manner that was his style. She always misinterpreted the praise as condescending "babying." During the interview, we elicited the facts that as the only daughter of a Southern family, she had never felt that her father accepted, recognized, or praised any of her extensive academic or professional achievements. As a child, she felt she was always in the position of having to prove herself. Laurie worked hard as an adolescent, planned well, and left home to go to an out-of-state college in the North when she was just sixteen.

Laurie reacted to Philip in this same manner. She saw him as being unaccepting. He fostered this projection by withholding serious praise and substituting jocularity, but at the same time all his actions indicated his faith in her abilities. Caught up in the position of the unaccepted daughter trying to win the approval of a demanding father, she interpreted all his actions in this light. She never broached the subject of her feelings with him. In fact, on the surface, they seemed to work together extremely well. One month after the initial interview, she confided to us that she had received another job offer and was leaving. She felt that since she was so unappreciated, she had little chance for advancement. Although from what many people at Redex told us, Laurie was definitely "on the way up" and highly regarded by upper-level management, she saw her situation in opposite terms. The same words and actions of her boss, which others knew to be praise, Laurie saw as indicative of failure. She felt she was being ignored or taken advantage of while everyone else thought she was being noticed.

How do we know that we are projecting onto our bosses and not simply seeing things as they really are? Why should we think we are dragging our childhood conflicts into the work place when we may be accurate in our evaluations? One good indication is our pattern of relating to authority. Many people repeatedly find themselves ending up in the same relationship with their managers, no matter how different these people may initially seem to be.

Perhaps they are always fearful and unable to voice any criticism. Perhaps they are always angry and resentful, unable to get along with them and angry at their power. They dream of the day they can rid themselves of that servile relationship and be "their own boss."

Many people find it difficult to have a relationship with their managers that they feel good about. They find their interactions unsatisfying and troubling but also very difficult to change. Projections are very hard to break. We are locked into seeing someone in a certain manner. Our perception of them is shaped by the force of our own very powerful emotions and needs. Yet it always seems to us that our feelings about them are caused by them, not by us.

This pattern of our reaction to authority is not limited to our work. It extends to the way we react to other "authority figures." In fact, it can be a useful and informative exercise to make a list of our most dominant feelings about policemen, for example, and compare it to a list of our feelings about our bosses. What you may find is that your reactions are very much the same. This is because the way we respond to people in different jobs and professions is determined as much by what we bring to the situation as by the actual qualities possessed by them. As an example, let us look at people's feelings about physicians. In our culture, doctors are accorded higher status than any other occupational group. Because they have certain abilities, training, and credentials, they are suitable targets for parental projections and even the mythic projections of the savior or the wise old man.

Many people endow their doctors with incredible powers, though their performance does not warrant it. They give great weight to the doctor's recommendations. They have to struggle to disobey "doctor's orders." Projection rather than accurate perception is what is responsible for so many people consulting their family doctors on the most personal matters, problems that are really far from their area of expertise. Many feel their doctors are experts in interpersonal relations, child rearing, and even financial matters.

Of course, many doctors cultivate themselves to be the perfect target for these projections—the white coat, the degrees on the walls, even the long (and often quite unnecessary) waiting to be allowed into the inner sanctum enhance this image and create the distance between doctor and patient in which the projection flourishes.

The feelings we have for doctors are extreme—unrealistically high because they go beyond stereotyping and into projection. When this projection breaks down—as it often does—the strength of the reaction is equal to the strength of the original projection. When we project a mythical image, we attribute too much credit to another. When the projection no longer fits the target and we do not understand this process, we blame the target for not containing the projection. The hatred and revulsion felt for the medical profession by many grows from this breakdown. "Doctors are not gods but money-hungry heartless villains, more concerned with their golf plans than with my life." The reaction is so strong because the disappointment at the inability of these people to hold the projection is so great.

Sibling Systems—Parallel Projections

The people we work with directly are often as or more important to us than the people we work for. These are the people with whom we have the most contact. If the boss holds the place of the parent at work, these people are our siblings.

"In any co-ordinated human activity," writes F. J. Rolthlisberger, "people belong to small work groups in which meaningful associations and activities take place. . . . In business each small work group has its technical and economic purpose in terms of which its members are formally related. But also each has its own informal codes of behavior which provide important functions for individuals and an effective basis for co-operation."[2]

Patty Lloyd is a technical writer at Redex. She works closely with three other technical writers and editors and two secretaries. Their division is a small world unto itself within the larger organization.

"I enjoy my job very much for two reasons: interesting work and interesting, friendly people. In particular, there are two women at work to whom I feel particularly close. It makes me feel very good to see that we can cooperate so well. I originally attributed this to a real identification—'sisterhood'—we would not allow male competitiveness to characterize our work relationships."

Patty is friendly with all the people in her division, but particularly so with Sandra, another technical writer. They are both the same age, both transplanted Midwesterners.

Most people seek out alliances at work. Small groups form, made up of people who are friendly with each other, who eat lunch together, who gossip together. It is useful to look at these coalitions as sibling groups, allied in separation from and often in antagonism against the parents.

We have a need to find a comfortable group at work, people with whom we can feel secure. This need leads us to see certain others as being like us, as sharing our feelings, as being motivated by similar energies. We project attitudes, feelings, and ideas that we know we have and that make up our conscious sense of ourselves upon some of our co-workers. Although we are conscious of the attitudes in ourselves, we are unaware that we are projecting them, quite unconscious that we are not seeing others as they are but only as we suppose them to be.

Who makes a good target for these kinds of projections? Many times, although certainly not necessarily, they are our peers, people who serve a similar function or who work at a similar level to ours. There are other factors, of course—age, sex, educational background—that make someone a good target. When we project similarity onto those in our immediate work group, we have created a convivial, pleasant work situation that fosters loyalty and cohesiveness. These feelings are often based more on illusion, on projection of our attitudes, than on reality. But they can continue and flourish if they are kept in the atmosphere in which they grow (the office) and are not transplanted to a less appropriate environment.

Patty told us the following episode about her relationship with Sandra:

"The funny thing is that while I feel close to Sandy, we can only be close at work. Once I invited her to spend a weekend afternoon with me. We had spoken so much about being working mothers that I really wanted to meet her children. But what happened was that I was very ill at ease. Somehow we didn't have much in common. Her house was very different than what I imagined it to be, and her husband—he was awful. I was shocked. It just didn't work out. We still are great co-workers, but I realize we don't have as much in common as I thought."

Within the controlled environment of work, we are able to sustain the parallel projection; the opportunity for it to break down is more limited. But seeing the person in a new circumstance can make its continuation difficult. Too many holes appear in the image; we are left with another person who looks very different from the one we thought we knew so well.

Clear-cut hierarchy often produces an atmosphere conducive to parallel projection. If things are set up so that one knows who one's peers are, who the superiors and subordinates are, and the routes up are clearly marked, parallel projection often occurs. This is because there are well-marked, appropriate targets. It is harder to form your own peer group than to work with one that already has a potential existence.

Unconscious Projections

"In the office in which I work, there are five people of whom I am afraid. Each of these five people is afraid of four people (including overlaps), for a total of twenty, and each of these twenty people is afraid of six people, making a total of one hundred and twenty people who are feared by at least one person.... I ... find it impossible to know exactly what is going on behind the closed doors of all the offices on all the floors occupied by all the people in this and all the other companies in the whole world who might say or do something, intentionally or circumstantially, that could bring me to ruin.... I have the feeling that someone nearby is soon going to find out something about me that will mean the end, although I can't imagine what that something is."[3]

Anyone who has ever worked in an office or other large organization will recognize the feelings of this character in Joseph Heller's novel, *Something Happened*.

What is happening when we see aggression, hostility, and peril all around us at work, but feel that we don't harbor these feelings ourselves? While many of us work in competitive environments, few people acknowledge that they have strong feelings of competition and hostility. We are repressing these impulses within ourselves so that we are unaware of them, and then we project them upon those around us. This insulates us from these feelings. We experience them as occurring "out there" in our work environment, not inside us.

The employees of the Sales Division at Redex have a hard job. Pharmaceuticals is a big and competitive business, and they must convince clients to buy Redex products while dealing with pressure from their managers to perform and sell. John Dorman spoke at length about his job. He has been selling for Redex for eight years and has his eye on a head-of-sales position for one of the best territories.

"I'm only doing my job. I personally don't wish harm to anyone. But the people around me—God! The other salesmen would like nothing better than to see me really screw up. I've really got to watch my step around here, play it close to the vest. For one thing, I keep to myself, *never* let them know about anything good opening up in the territory, for instance. Basically I'm an easygoing guy, but I've learned my lesson."

While, like John, we refuse to acknowledge "socially undesirable" feelings such as hostility, aggression, or strong competition, we become acutely aware of those feelings in others. When people complain about their co-workers, they may really be describing themselves. When they repress impulses and then project them, they become "sensitized to"—that is, extremely aware of—that repressed quality in others. The energy of that repressed impulse makes itself felt in other ways. John sees hostility and aggression in many of the people around him. But he doesn't view himself as a competitive or hostile person.

In extreme forms, when someone completely represses strong aggressive feelings, we have the perfect stage set for paranoia; the world is seen as a hostile and treacherous environment fraught with peril. It is a well-documented psychological phenomenon that frustration is related to aggression and hostility.[4] Many jobs are full of frustration, which engenders hostility. However, the work place—especially one placing a high value upon "professionalism"—is not considered the place for its expression. So it comes out in a different form—in projection.

The Scapegoat

Sociologists and psychologists have shown that there is a relationship between economic conditions, frustration, and scapegoating. For example, one study indicated that as the price of cotton in the South went down, the number of lynchings of blacks went up.[5] Similarly, high work tension can also lead to an intensification of scapegoating phenomenon.

The Technical Writing department of which Patty is a member also includes an editorial staff. Edith, Lorraine, and Sandra are the three copyeditors at Redex. Their services are used by a number of departments, primarily by Technical Writing and Public Relations. At certain times, there are high demands on their time by both departments. There are deadlines to meet, high work volume, and, consequently, high pressure.

Lorraine Sopon is the chief editor. A woman in her mid-forties, she was hired on the recommendation of a friend of the president

of Redex. Her frowsy brown hair, mismatched clothes, and frequently flushed face after a few lunchtime cocktails combine to
make her look rather unkempt. Lorraine is known throughout
Redex, and from what we heard, she is disliked. But among her
immediate co-workers, she is the object of rather intense dislike
and contempt.

Edith, the copyeditor who has worked at the company for many
years, spoke to us about her supervisor. "Lorraine Sopon is a dis-
credit to the profession. She is selfish, uncaring, and a slob. It is
discouraging and depressing. She can degrade me because she
does my evaluations. She *almost* had me to the point where *I* was
questioning my ability, but not quite. She is always trying to get
other people to do things for her. We are always having to cover
up her mistakes, do her work. The thing about her is that she
doesn't care at all about the end product, being a good editor.
She's dumb, not conscientious. She just knows enough to rely on
all the others of us to cover up for her."

The qualities of the scapegoat that are infinitely irritating are
almost always those very qualities we do not acknowledge in ourselves. Lorraine is hated because she is uncaring, sloppy, undisciplined—all characteristics that are unacceptable in editors but
that they all possess to some degree. Rather than acknowledge
their own failings, the less competent editor becomes the perfect
target for the projections of these negative, undesirable traits. It
is often quite instructive to list all the things we really can't stand
about someone else. The chances are that we will learn more about
ourselves than about them.

In all probability, the target does possess the negative qualities
to some extent. But our involvement with them, our horrified
fascination, our endless annoyance, are clear indications of
projection. We are caught up with the scapegoat because we are
seeing parts of ourselves in them. That is why it is so hard to dis-
engage from the other person, to "just forget about him" and get
on with our work.

Almost everyone in the editorial, technical writing, and public-
relations departments agrees on the opinion of Lorraine. This is a
diverse group of people who have to work together. Although they
would all say Lorraine stands in the way of them accomplishing
their goals, she really helps them by creating a feeling of group
cohesion and unity.

As the parallel projection of positive qualities seems to unite a
group, so too does the unconscious projection of negative qualities

onto the scapegoat provide unity. The tension and pressure of the work place become focused in a way that leads to harmony within the group. Agreement on the "villain" unifies people, accentuating their solidarity and similarity and directing attention from other differences and problems that might exist.

A great deal of "office politics" involves plotting to rid everyone of the hated person. But when such plots succeed, the resulting atmosphere is not significantly improved. Quite the contrary; often things are more chaotic than before. Quickly enough, someone else turns up as the scapegoat. Often when a scapegoat leaves the group, someone who at one time was acceptable takes his place. This confirms that it is largely projections that determine the pariah.

An accurate way to understand the changes that take place in a work group over time is in terms of the shift in targets for the projection of the group's hostility. Robert's description of current developments in the political machinations of the Research Department brought this out clearly to us.

"When I arrived at Redex Research, there was a great deal of in-fighting. I had heard about office politics in graduate school, but it seemed that in this department, the most important variable determining status and promotion was which side you were on. After several uncomfortable years, a few angry members left, and there was a change in the manager. This guy Paul really supported everyone in the department and led us effectively whenever we ran into snags with the top management. They were attempting to reorganize, cut back on our support staff. We felt that management was at fault for our declining profits and that we were paying the price. The only thing that made the situation bearable was that we all felt the same way. It took a couple of years, but eventually the key management people were replaced and Redex entered a period of financial growth. Shortly thereafter, our manager, Paul, told us that he was leaving and returning to an academic position because he couldn't stand the business world any more. Now we get along with top management, but we're having a lot of trouble with our support staff."

It makes sense that if a scapegoat leaves, a replacement is quickly found, since the scapegoat serves such an important function both for the individuals and the group. In the initial group structure he described, the hostility was focused within. This was followed by researchers and management becoming opposing factions. This is the typical structure of opposing groups scapegoating each other. The significant change in group structure occurred when the hostility was focused outside the immediate group. We can imagine members plotting against various upper-level managers and finding themselves in harmonious agreement. Once the upper-level managers left, new avenues for the expression of aggression had to be found. It would appear to us that Paul was leaving because the group structure could no longer be so easily maintained by projecting upon upper-level management scapegoats. It would seem that although having a scapegoat in our midst can cause problems, not having one can create even more problems.

Lisa works as a lab technician in Redex's lab testing section. "There are thirty people in my division," she says. "They are all 'techs.' There is no actual hierarchical distinction among them, but there certainly are more favored jobs to be given and higher salaries to be accrued.

"The more favored jobs involve working with the more sophisticated equipment and doing more complicated tests. There are also undue differences in the amount of money people are getting to do what are essentially the same jobs. But there are no clear-cut ways to move up with these. I found this very upsetting. The way to get these things on the job is by 'getting to' the boss—it seems mostly through personal contact and that's all.

"Another thing is that it is really very important for people to cooperate with each other. We are dealing with what could be very dangerous chemicals if they are not handled properly, and we all share all the equipment and glassware. This means that everyone has got to clean up the glassware and put their chemicals away. There's always potential for danger. But the amazing thing is that people don't cooperate. Although it is dangerous to be inconsiderate, people are anyway. There are many, many small cliques within the group, but these don't really have any stability. They are always changing around. No one seems to have any loyalty to anyone else. The only thing that doesn't change is the amount of gossip. People are always gossiping about each other, all the time. Someone's always afraid someone else is taking advantage of them, or lying to them, or not telling them something. It's constant and I can't stand it. People are just hurtful to each other and petty.

"Sometimes everyone really gets down on one person if they are being particularly sloppy—at lunch, there will be a lot of complaining, although no one will ever confront that person. There just tends to be a lot of griping."

This work situation is full of frustration—poor, crowded work conditions that make completion of tasks difficult; very ill-defined lines of ascent; lack of cooperation when cooperation is sorely needed to complete tasks adequately. There is a great deal of tension that arises from the physical dangers inherent in the job and the lack of certainty about the routes of advancement. People's anger doesn't get projected onto any one target but swirls around, settling and resettling on various hooks. This is a definite contrast to the editorial department we just described. There the work tensions were resolved. When there is a clear scapegoat, it is as though the whole group holds up a prism through which the sum of everyone's negativity, frustration, hostility, and insecurity is focused in one beam and projected upon one target. As we saw, this focusing leads to greater harmony. In the lab situation, all the negative energy is free-floating.

Projection Breakdown

The projection of hostility onto one particular person within the group is not the only kind of projection that changes over time. Projections dissolve and shift on the job for many reasons. If we become conscious of possessing a quality that we have been projecting, we may no longer need to project it; or people may be hired who are better targets for various projections. As we come to know people a little better, it may become more difficult to maintain the tie between projection and person.

Earlier, we saw how parallel projections were threatened when someone we interviewed invited her co-worker home. The feelings of compatibility, sameness, and comfort were placed in doubt. It is also apparent that our projections onto the boss don't last forever. In fact, it seems that Americans are finding it harder to maintain parent projections onto a manager or boss. As in entertainment and politics, we seem to become disillusioned more quickly.

Janet DeWitt works with the president of Redex as an executive assistant. She told the following story, which captures the sudden breakdown of a projection. "At about three thirty, the alarms started going off. At first, everyone ignored them, but they just kept going. After about a minute, I started getting those same *Towering Inferno* images in my head that I was sure everyone else had. I was starting to get a little nervous. I walked over to the person at the next desk, 'Do you think we should leave?'

" 'I don't know. I'd like to finish this report.'

" 'I know, but the alarms keep going.'

" 'All right. But let's not take the elevator. In case this is for real, I think the fire stairs. And let's check with Charles [the boss].'

"Just then, Charles came out of his office, asking, 'Where is everybody going? It's a damn drill and there is an enormous amount of work to do. Everybody stay put and I'll call and check to see what's really going on.' Charles went back into his private office, but after a few minutes everyone started leaving.

"We started down the fifteen flights, meeting up with others along the way. I didn't smell smoke but I started going down quickly. Then I smelled it. Definitely smoke. I really got scared. I expected to be trampled by the hordes. We all got downstairs and milled around outside. A few minues later, as the fire engines were driving up, Charles emerged from the building half-jogging.

"It was all over before long. We didn't even get the afternoon off. It turned out to be a wastebasket fire in a men's bathroom on the fourth floor. Everyone was joking as we waited to get an elevator to our floor back upstairs. People milled around a bit but quickly got back to work. I tried but it was hard to concentrate. One thing that changed as a result of that incident was my view of Charles. When he got back upstairs, he joked a bit about all the fuss over nothing, but he really blew it. He looked older, and what I used to think was distinguished now looked phony. The memory of him hustling out of the building with one hand over his tie to keep it from waving over his shoulder seemed ludicrous. For me, he just doesn't command the same respect he once did."

The New York Times reported in March, 1981, that "Today, a new and edgy atmosphere haunts America's executive suites."[6] This is due in large part to the shaky state of the economy. A father has to be able to provide for the family, and if he cannot, there seems to be little room for loyalty. David Jays, an executive recruiter, said, "I think a higher set of expectations is created when a company goes outside (which is occurring more and more). The thinking becomes, 'We've scoured the country. We've chosen this guy from dozens. He must be superman.' And when he isn't, things can go sour very quickly." Jays has described the process of this type of projection breakdown, and as the *Times* story reports, "Top managers—presidents and chief executives—seem to be getting dismissed more frequently, more publicly, and after much shorter tenures than ever before."[7]

It seems that the expectations others have of these top executives are very unrealistic. Decisions to hire and to fire are not made on purely logical, "business" grounds. In times of high stress due to economic pressures, there is a heavy emotional component to these decisions. Part of what is going on is the projection onto these executives of images they cannot possibly hold. Conditions are bad, and therefore the amount of time it takes for the gap to appear between the person and the projection is short.

Although our projections at work do break down, they can continue for long periods of time. While this produces a stable atmosphere, the target of these long-term projections may begin to feel burdened by them.

"I'm Tired of My Job"

People's feelings about their jobs evolve and change over the course of time. Often the way the people we interviewed described the ebb and flow of these emotions sounded very much like the story of a love affair.

When we first take on a new job, we are acquiring a whole new role, and this role makes us the target for an entire set of projections. Much of the excitement and enjoyment that are first experienced at a new job comes from the enjoyment we get from having a "new image," that is, bearing new projections.

When the kinds of projections we receive from others are positive—when we are seen as brilliant, masterful, competent, and collected—we are energized. Often people report that what most excited them about a better job or a promotion is the change in the way they are seen by others.

The excitement that comes with being the target of others' projections fades over time, and usually we have no idea why what used to make us feel good no longer does.

A well-known psychologist and psychotherapist told us that he did not enjoy teaching and had no interest in ever teaching at a university. "At first, I worked to be both entertaining and profound, and shortly the students loved me. I began to feel quite lonely. I tried to make myself known to them, but they wouldn't have it. To them, I was a magical figure. They adored me. It was terribly isolating—horrible."

Many of us might have trouble understanding how someone could feel so bad about being adored or loved. This psychologist had enough basic self-esteem so that he did not truly need the adoration of these students. He also was aware that they weren't really seeing him but were amazed by their own projections. His attempts at developing a more realistic relationship were unsuccessful. He felt unknown. It seems that although it may be great to be admired, if we realize that it is not *we* who are the object of affection but rather an image, it is not satisfying.

If people are projecting their own images, feelings, and needs upon you, no matter how positive these may be, the end result is never completely satisfying. Only some aspects of your personality are being seen. Undeniably people want to be known and accepted for themselves, not for an image. Projections are not nourishing because they don't recognize the whole person.

On the job, many of us reach a point where we just aren't happy with our situation. We long for a change even when things seem to be going well. Whether or not we are the objects of positive or negative projections, we all reach this point. We can always change jobs and set the whole process in motion again. Or we can find new ways of relating to the people around us, ways in which the images can break down and dialogue between real people can occur.

One contact at Redex was a friend of ours, Diana, a mid-level executive in the Finance Department. She had been doing very well at her work until a new vice-president was appointed to head her division. Diana just couldn't get along with him. She certainly tried. It was very important to her career that she be able to work with this man. But he really annoyed and upset her. Even when she left the office, she couldn't get him out of her mind. She found him incredibly aggressive and manipulative. She resented the way he dealt with her and with the rest of the staff.

We suggested to Diana that when someone really "gets under your skin," the cause very well might be projection. We suggested she might try the technique of *projection identification* as a way of dealing with her feelings about the vice-president. If projections were at work, this would be a way of recognizing and taking them back. One way to do this is to make a list of all the qualities that describe the person you're having trouble with. That is, write a little sketch. We suggested this to Diana in the hope that by doing this, she would discover parts of herself that she had difficulty getting in touch with. Our assumption was that it was those unowned parts of herself that she was projecting onto her boss. We suggested that she think about these traits as though they were hers.

Diana told us that she tried the exercise and came up with the following list: greedy, selfish, superior, and particularly competitive. This was very interesting, because Diana has always been one of the most even-tempered people we know. She prides herself on maintaining her integrity and sense of fairness in the very competitive field she's in. It became clear that she had repressed many of the feelings she felt were negative, such as anger, competitiveness, jealousy. What she saw in the vice-president were all these in an exaggerated form. By really articulating what it is about someone that you're having trouble with, and thinking about what those qualities mean to you, you have a technique for getting a clearer perspective on what's really going on in the problem relationship.

A few weeks later, Diana told us she had an argument with the vice-president over an important account. At first, we were concerned, but she told us that it really cleared the air. He was, in fact, pleased that she was so assertive and was glad she could defend her point of view.

She was able to deal with him effectively because she wasn't caught up in feeling furious with him. She felt she could see him more clearly for what he really was. She still doesn't particularly like him, but he doesn't drive her crazy anymore. We think it's because she is better able to separate who he is from who she is.

Psychologists are often asked the difficult question, "What does it mean to be a healthy person?" Freud was reported to have said that a healthy person is one who can love and work. This may sound like a simplistic answer, but we believe this statement says much more than the pages of definitions found in clinical-psychology textbooks. To love and work successfully means one has to be relatively free of inner conflict. Anxiety and depression, for example, impede our ability to function well with people in or out of work. Our outer conflicts mirror our inner ones. People unable to perform on the job often cannot get along with others because they are blinded and burdened by their projections.

We spend so much time with people at work that it is one of the best opportunities to discover ourselves and develop healthy relationships. We need to examine our intense emotional reactions to the people around us. Why do we find the boss so frightening or despicable? Why do we feel infatuated with someone we barely know? What makes a co-worker so hated? Why do we get excited by a promotion or feel tired of our position? The answers lie in the unrecognized parts of ourselves that we see in others, or in their projections onto us.

7

Stars and Fans

On June 22, 1981, Mark David Chapman pleaded guilty to a second-degree-murder charge. He admitted shooting John Lennon in the outdoor foyer of The Dakota apartment house on Central Park West with thirty-eight-caliber hollow-point bullets "to ensure John Lennon's death."[1] To the surprise of most of the stunned world, the killer was an ardent fan of his victim.

John W. Hinckley composed a one-and-a-half-page letter to Jodi Foster. "Dear Jodi," he wrote, "There is a definite possibility that I will be killed in my attempt to get Reagan. As you know by now, I love you very much. The past months I have left you dozens of poems, letters and messages in the faint hope you would develop an interest in me ... I would abandon this idea of getting Reagan in a second if I could only win your heart and live out the rest of my life with you." He signed the letter "I love you forever."[2] It is dated 12:45 P.M., March 30, 1981, a few months after Lennon had been murdered and an hour and forty-five minutes before the President was shot.

Early in his career, Freud recognized that there is no discontinuity between normal and abnormal behavior. What we consider to be psychopathological is simply an exaggeration of the normal. For example, everyone feels nervous from time to time or too jittery to sleep. But in someone suffering from an anxiety disorder, this normal tendency is intensified until the anxiety is so debilitating that normal functioning is impaired. Similarly, everyone occasionally feels let down or sad. The depressed person may feel this to such an extreme that he is unable to get out of bed or dress himself. By studying anxiety disorders or depression, we gain a better understanding of nervousness or sadness in "normal people." One of the reasons psychologists study abnormal behavior is that it is an exaggeration of the normal. This magnification makes our study and understanding of human nature easier. Chapman's and Hinckley's behavior are magnifications of normal fan reaction.

Fan is short for *fanatic*, a word that derives from *fanaticus*, meaning "someone inspired to frenzy by devotion to a deity."[3] Both Chapman and Hinckley certainly live up to this definition. Their names will always be linked to those of their idols. And although they would be considered abnormal by most clinicians, the ways in which they related to their idols exemplify in extreme form the two most important fan-star relationships existing in our culture.

1. John Lennon was Mark Chapman's *hero*, a man he worshiped in a way that far exceeded the admiration most of us feel for our own heroes. The average person might strive to emulate or proclaim devotion by wearing T-shirts emblazoned with their heroes' faces, buying every record, watching every performance "religiously." But Chapman took his devotion to its extreme, to that place where he no longer could separate himself from his hero, to a place where he signed himself as "John Lennon." And to achieve a final bond, he murdered him—ensuring that their destinies would always be linked.

2. Many of us who have fallen in love know that we would do almost anything to attract our new love—buying new clothes, changing our "image," scheming and planning. If our tactics don't succeed, we are crushed. Although Hinckley's trial has revealed his many plans and motives, one theme remains dominant: he was totally infatuated with Jodi Foster. She was his *dream girl*, his ideal woman. But his frenzied attempt to win her led him to the same extreme as Mark Chapman—to a place where most of us will never go.

The Projection of the Archetypal Image

For Jung, an archetypal image is one that influences, impresses and fascinates us. This is the hold entertainers exert on us. "The concept of the archetype ... is derived from the repeated observation that, for instance, the myths and fairytales of world literature contain definite motifs which crop up everywhere. We meet these same motifs in the fantasies, dreams, deliria and delusions of individuals living today."[4] Among the most common and important mythic images are the hero and the dream girl or dream boy. For thousands of years, the targets of these projections were in religious and mythological systems. The ancient Greeks had great heroes like Perseus, Hercules, and Odysseus and archetypal lovers such as Paris, Aphrodite, and Helen to hold the projected images. In the medieval period, there was a rich Christian religious tradition as well as the mythos of courtly love as exemplified by Arthur and the knights and Sir Gawain. Compared to the stories of mythological figures of earlier times, the current culture is barren. The earlier systems have lost their power to carry or hold our projections. But we have not lost the need for targets for these archetypal images. Jung suggests that we all have the potential to develop our own anima or animus or hero archetype. However, if we have not developed and incorporated the qualities that belong to these archetypes into our personalities (and most of us have not), we must project them.

Where do our gods and goddesses reside? There seems no doubt that our Mt. Olympus is in Hollywood, with satellite colonies on Broadway and playing fields around the country. We truly idolize and worship the actors, musicians, and athletes. Because these are the targets that are shared by so many of us, not only have we found suitable hooks on which to hang our mythic projections, we also experience a sense of community in shared worship.

The Adolescent Fan

Before the Beatles ever arrived in the United States, before fans in America had ever seen them, a New York radio station blared, "It is now 6:50 P.M. Beatle time. They left London thirty minutes ago. They're out over the Atlantic Ocean, headed for New York. The temperature is thirty-two Beatle degrees." When the Beatles arrived at Kennedy airport, there were more fans than the Beatles had ever seen before. As described by P. Norman in the book *Shout:*

> Screaming, they hung over balconies and retaining walls; screaming, they buckled against a hundred-man police cordon, oblivious to peril or pain. . . . As the Beatles, somnambulistically, began to descend the steps a girl on the terminal's outside level flung herself into space and hung there on the arms of two companions crying, "Here I am!"[5]

Adolescent fans are very open about their projections, although they certainly don't call their involvement with their favorite stars by such a name. The projection of the dream figure and hero are quite common at this age. It is a normal and in fact healthy occurrence, acting as a bridge that eases the transition from child to adult.

During childhood, the dream figure and hero images are unknown, buried deep within the unconscious. A child has no inkling of the hero within but will become fascinated with a knight, a cowboy, an athlete, or a spaceman. It is usually at early adolescence that the dream archetypes are externalized, projected, and thus discovered. At this point in our development, we are not ready to incorporate these aspects of ourselves. But we are ready and eager to meet them.

The adolescent is the most passionate type of fan in our culture. But there are clear sex differences when it comes to the kinds of targets with which boys and girls become so intensely involved. The girls focus on the so-called teen idols. One generation of girls screamed for Sinatra, the next for Presley, and the next for the Beatles. Today's teenage girls send love letters to Matt Dillon, Timothy Hutton, Leif Garret, and a few others. They write, "I love you, please send me your autographed picture." They rarely indicate they want to date, meet, or even see their idols. A fan cannot be hurt or disappointed by a photograph. She can have a perfect and beautiful romance with a fantasy.

Linda Watson, the entertainment editor of *Teen Magazine*, told us that the girls between twelve and fifteen were the most extreme fans she heard from. They seemed to be most attracted to pretty rather than macho faces. The teen idols, she told us, almost always appeared somewhat feminine. "They almost always have long hair and look cute and friendly. I think these girls are somewhat insecure and prefer men who are clearly not threatening or frightening. They want to know about their idol's home life, what they eat, how they sleep, what they like and don't like, etcetera, but they don't really want to get too close."

Teenage girls often have strong, meaningful friendships with other girls, but they have problems building relationships with males. They do have crushes on real boys, but most often the boys are older, in higher grades—in short, unattainable. When a teenage girl wants an intimate relationship with a male but is not ready for one, she will make one up. This fantasy relationship can be with a boy in the neighborhood or a teen idol. By finding out everything about the habits of the idol, the fantasy relationship can take some form and substance. In this way, a teenage girl may satisfy a need until she is mature enough to develop a more real relationship.

Adolescence is a very difficult time for all members of the family, not only the adolescent. Everything is in flux—the parents must redefine their relationship to each other as the child prepares to leave childhood and become an adult. In order to leave home, the child must successfully develop the qualities and abilities that will allow her to care for herself, to become an independent human being. A typical phase in this development is the search outside herself for the means of deliverance from the family to the "real world." The growing abilities and qualities that will eventually enable her to leave are projected outside, onto a "prince charming," the animus figure. This prince is gallant, independent, assertive, and has the necessary transportation (horse or car) to take her out of the family home and into the world.

What are the twelve- to eighteen-year-old boys projecting while the girls are discovering their prince charmings? There is relatively little projection of the anima onto female entertainers at this age. Once in a while, a boy will express interest in a female star. But the reaction seems to be mild compared with their female counterparts. Teenage boys have also been very involved with Presley, the Beatles, and others, but the nature of their archetypal projections is different. They do not see dream lovers; they see heroes. Actors and musicians receive many hero projections from young boys, but the primary targets are athletes.

In the fanatical world of the sports fan, the most avid fans are the adolescent boys. Their involvement with their favorite athletes exceeds that of almost all adults. Theirs is a special type of infatuation. They wear shirts with their favorite's name and number. They follow their exploits every day with relentless perseverance and dedication. Often they are capable of reciting unbelievable amounts of numbers and statistics. Boys are often so involved with these hero figures that they celebrate when they win and mourn when they lose. "His victory" becomes "my victory": "We won last night."

This "hero worship" serves a valuable psychological function. Although the adolescent boy is not yet ready to take on the struggles and battles of adulthood, by projecting the hero within, those heroic qualities are met, recognized, and examined. Adolescent girls too have the potential to project a hero image, but in our culture, few targets have been available. This situation seems to be changing. Many teenage girls have found hero images in Billy Jean King, Chris Evert, and Olga Korbet.

The recollections of one thirty-year-old woman about the Beatles seemed to us to be a good summary of our findings on the adolescent fan: "The Beatles took over the US when I was twelve. During the next year or so, every junior high school girl and a lot of boys had their favorite Beatle. The true romantics among the girls favored Paul McCartney and wore buttons on their coats proclaiming 'I love Paul.' There were many who seriously dreamed of marrying him! George Harrison attracted the shy, quiet types and those boys who appreciated the fact that he was the best guitarist. 'I love George' was their button. John Lennon was for the intellectuals of both sexes, and with the exception of a few girls who went for his sense of humor or preferred not to run with the 'Paul' faction, these fans disdained the button-wearing form of adulation. Later, when John became political, teenage boys who jeered at the earlier hero worship now joined the Lennon camp. Ringo had a far smaller but quite distinct following; the sort of girl who was crazy about stray animals, for instance. They went for 'Ringo' buttons in a big way."

Adult Fans

As long as we project our mythical images, their qualities, power, and energy are not ours but reside in the objects of our fascination. However, because the work of internalizing them is quite difficult, most of us continue in our projections.

As adults, we may stop talking endlessly about our favorite celebrity; their pictures are no longer on our bedroom walls; we have ceased keeping scrapbooks or collecting memorabilia. But we are still fans and the process is the same as it was when we were younger.

Outside virtually every Broadway theater, there are groups of adult fans waiting for a glimpse of their idol. Every major entertainer gets thousands of pieces of mail containing presents, professions of love, and proposals of marriage. Every day adults get their pictures taken with their favorite star at the Hollywood Wax Museum. Millions of adults place their emotional lives in the hands of an athlete.

Although they are absorbed in fantasy relationships, teenage fans seem to distinguish the entertainers from the character they are playing. Adult fans sometimes have a harder time. Their projections continue well after the show is over. Adult TV fans attack villainous characters in public places. They send wedding presents to characters on shows. (When Rhoda, the TV character played by Valerie Harper, got married, the studio received an unprecedented number of gifts and telegrams.) When favorite characters are in financial difficulty, fans actually send cash and checks.

Projections work miracles. They transform characters into real people, wax dummies into exciting personalities, sweaty athletes into heroes, toads into princes, and entertainers into extraordinary gods and goddesses. Based on our discussions with movie critics, fan-magazine writers, and entertainment editors, we learned how intense fan reactions can be. The difference between an extreme fan and the rest of us is not as great as we'd like to think. Most of us do not write letters or get our pictures taken with wax dummies, but we are taken with stars in a way that goes far beyond their talent or ability; we are infatuated with them. James Seymour, an editor of *People* magazine, said, "For some people it's the Fonz or Farrah Fawcett, while for others it's a dancer, poet or philosopher, but always there's a type of idealization that makes us all fans." The results of our survey seem to support this view.

The Survey

We took an opinion sample of 100 adults, asking them to answer the following two questions:

1. Who is your favorite male actor, singer, or entertainer? Why is he your favorite and what specifically do you like about him?
2. Who is your favorite female actress, singer, or entertainer? Why is she your favorite and what specifically do you like about her?

We were interested primarily in the reasons that a normal adult group of people would present for *why* they like particular entertainers. Do their reasons indicate that projections are at work? If so, what are the nature of these projections and do they change according to age and sex? When we started, we were not sure what to expect, but what emerged was a pattern of responses indicating that favored entertainers receive basic types of projections: the dream lover and the hero. We project the hero archetype onto the favorite entertainer of the same sex and the dream figure onto the favorite entertainer of the opposite sex. This pattern is consistent with the mythic projections of Chapman and Hinckley.

Only one of the participants said he liked "no one in particular" and had "no one favorite." Most people have focused attention on one entertainer as special.

Because we live in an era of media saturation and are supplied with a multitude of targets for our projections, it was not surprising that no one celebrity dominated the polling. Yet the descriptions of these various favored entertainers are remarkably similar. It is projection that plays a large role in creating our responses or feelings about these stars. Though talent plays a part, very few people mentioned that they selected a favorite entertainer because of acting ability or technique, or a favorite musician because of the sound or quality of the voice or the ability to play an instrument.

The Hero: Entertainers of the Same Sex

The Greek word for *hero* means "the embodiment of composite ideals." The hero is the man or woman who leaves his own world and enters a region where battle must be done with incredible foes.* When they return in triumph, their victory benefits others as well as themselves. The image of the hero has always been that of a strong, brave, courageous, idealistic, independent, persevering person. The fight is a battle with evil, and this evil assumes many forms—dragon, demon, gangster, "bad guys."

When we looked at the predominant reasons women gave for their selection of a favorite actress, talent, technique, and ability were not the major factors. Although mentioned, they were secondary to personality descriptions emphasizing a strong, independent woman who triumphed over great odds, who had the will to be herself—descriptions of a hero.

Women's Favorite Female Entertainers

"Sophia Loren is intelligent, beautiful, aging with great charm and grace. She seems to become more lovely as she grows older. I have always been impressed by her range of ability. I suppose I have also sympathized with her personal life and admire what she has achieved as a self-educated woman." (F, 38)

"I think that the type of songs that Judy Collins sings say a lot

---

* We are using the word *hero* to mean either a man or a woman. *Heroine* has connotations of the woman rescued rather than the rescuer.

about her views of life. She sings of love, caring, understanding, and accepting others and fighting for what you believe in. She is an independent woman who has gone her own way and made it on her own and I respect her for that." (F, 31)

"Besides the fact that I am completely awed by Katharine Hepburn's amazing talent, I admire her strength of character and the individualism she maintains. She has never conformed to the stereotyped weak female but has gone her own way." (F, 20)

"Debbie Harry started in the entertainment field at the bottom in Soho. She really went to the 'school of tough knocks.' But she held in there even though she had an extremely tough life. She knew she had talent and finally that talent got recognized." (F, 22)

"Bette Midler is my favorite. She does what she wants, how she wants—she doesn't compromise—and she just doesn't care what the world thinks. She did her same act when people didn't recognize her, before she became a star. I think everything she does in a performance is more for self-expression than it is for audience approval. She shapes the audience—they don't shape her. She's strong enough to be herself." (F, 33)

Even in a group notorious for its obsession with "image," among entertainers, Barbra Streisand is considered extreme. She exercises final control over every frame of her films—not a profile shot goes by that hasn't been approved. Over the past few years, she has definitely shifted her image. In her earliest movies, she always played the classic heroine. She was a Cinderella—the girl next door who magically becomes transformed into a princess or swan and marries the prince—Omar Shariff, Ryan O'Neal, Robert Redford. When Streisand realized women were less fascinated by this fairy tale, she began to change her image, playing more assertive, persevering, career-oriented women. She began singing more rock than pop. By following the shift in women's life goals, she was also trying to maintain her fans' projections. She has been quite successful at doing so.

In our opinion survey, more women selected Barbra Streisand than any other as their favorite female entertainer. Her enduring popularity is largely a result of her being able to change her image so as to continue to receive intense projections.

Men's Favorite Male Entertainer

The results of our survey indicate that there is something to the notions of a "man's man" and a "woman's woman." Just as Streisand was most favored by women and not mentioned by men, so

Clint Eastwood was most favored by the men and not mentioned by the women in our sample. And yet the descriptions of the favored entertainer of the same sex are similar. Men even more clearly project the image of the hero onto their favorite male entertainer. Here are some examples.

"Clint Eastwood is my favorite. He is quiet and tough. Although his recent movies are silly, I still think this way about him." (M, 19)

"I like Clint Eastwood because of his manner of enforcing justice. I like his style." (M, 21)

"I love Clint Eastwood in most of his movies. He is usually a macho, courageous, violent good guy, a vigilante who is up against incredible odds (the bad guys). Eastwood always wins, often an incredible struggle." (M, 20)

"My favorite is Charles Bronson. He has courage and he doesn't fear anything. He reminds me of myself." (M, 23)

Men don't say, I like so and so because the character he plays is tough, resilient, and overcomes all obstacles to be victorious. They seem to feel that the actor *is* the character. By playing certain roles consistently, actors run the risk of being typecast, but they also create a reliable image that can be used as a target for projections.

Aside from the physical power that is seen in the descriptions of their favorite actors, many men also project the qualities of the rebel—daring, willingness not to conform, courage to be an individual—onto their favorite stars. Said one: "My favorite is Elvis Costello. He rebels against the glitter and phoniness of his art form." (M, 18)

And from someone a bit older: "Elvis Presely was the only person to really change the way people entertained the audience by using body rhythms and 'letting loose.' He was a very kind person who really never thought that he was great, but he is The King." (M, 31)

The image of the hero projected by men onto their favorite entertainers is so striking that it was almost surprising that no one mentioned Superman, Batman, The Lone Ranger, or Rocky as his favorite. A few selected less macho types, and one respondent chose Fred Astaire. It's not that gentler, less assertive performers aren't liked by men, but they are not their *favorites*.

Many men project the hero image onto a sports figure. They continue fanatical relationships begun in childhood. Many people are depressed for days when their favorite athlete or team of athletes loses and manic when they win. This emotional flux is connected to our projections of the hero onto our favored athletes. The problem with all such projections is that someone else's battles and struggles are important, interesting, often all-consuming, and we neglect our own—the hero within.

The Dream Lover: Entertainers of the Opposite Sex

"According to Jung, "Anima and Animus [are] the personification of the feminine nature of a man's unconscious and the masculine nature of a woman's. . . . [They] manifest themselves most typically in personified form as figures in dreams and fantasies or in the irrationalities of a man's feelings and a woman's thinking. As regulators of behavior they are two of the most influential archetypes."[6]

The Animus Figure

What is the nature of the animus—the image of the dream boy—that is so fascinating to a woman, that has for centuries impressed and influenced her? According to Emma Jung, the animus has four principal characteristics: power, deed, word, and meaning. Rather than perceive these attributes in herself, many women transfer or project them onto a man who resembles this image. The four characteristics follow a developmental sequence. For a younger woman, physical prowess is the predominant aspect of the projected animus, whereas for a more mature woman, deeds, actions, and accomplishments are more important. Later in development, the ability to use words—an intellectual capacity— becomes the captivating aspect of the animus. The final aspect of the animus is meaning or wisdom.

Many women project the animus image onto a man they know, and this creates "together with an apparent satisfaction and completeness, a kind of compulsive tie to the man in question and a dependence on him that often increases to the point of becoming unbearable."[7] As we saw in Chapter 5, no individual man is ever capable of holding such a projection. This creates confusion and disappointment. Instead of working on developing the qualities of this inner figure ourselves, one way out is to project the qualities onto someone who cannot disappoint us—someone strong, successful, or brilliant whom we will never meet except in our dreams or in the movies.

What women see in their favorite male entertainer is the projection of the animus. Some are less sophisticated, focusing on physical appearance and strength; others more developed are impressed by word and wisdom. "David Bowie is sexy, has a great voice, and is quite mysterious not to mention a good Broadway actor. I think I'd like to date a man like him," said one respondent. (F, 22)

"Dennis Cole is gorgeous and he becomes completely engrossed in the role he is playing. He is blond and always has a tan." (F, 19)

"Mick Jagger is someone very special. He keeps putting out music that people listen to. There is just something about him. He has an energy which pulls you in. He is mysterious but accessible." (F, 31)

"I love Cary Grant's suave manners, especially the way he is with women. He is extremely handsome and his voice is very sexy. He appears to be so romantic on the screen." (F, 22)

"Jackson Browne's songs always relate to events that happen in my love life. I feel tuned in to him. He's also nice-looking and has a good voice." (F, 28)

"Robert Redford is extremely good-looking, versatile in his business, intelligent, talented, and sexually a turn-on." (F, 30)

"Mikhail Baryshnikov is talented technically, extremely gifted both physically and mentally. He is a complete thrill to watch." (F, 30)

"George C. Scott is a pleasure to watch because he has a combination of qualities which move me, touch me, sometimes excite me. His presence is powerful, emotional, sexual, and at the same time sensitive and gentle. And all the while, somewhere behind the eyes, there is this detached amusement—as if he knows something truer than what he says and does. I always try to see if he'll reveal it." (F, 43)

The male's favorite male entertainer is a hero figure, while the woman's favorite male entertainer is an animus figure. The animus seems quite competent, capable of handling a great variety of situations although not necessarily with brute force. The projected animus is strong, yet the strength is expressed subtly and often mysteriously. The animus is also knowing. The strength and knowledge of this image seem to be most often expressed in the "eyes." The women in our sample mentioned their favorite male star's eyes more often than any other part of the body.

The Anima Figure

"Every man carries with him the eternal image of woman, not the image of this or that particular woman, but a definitive feminine image," stated C. G. Jung. "This image is fundamentally unconscious, an hereditary factor of primordial origin engraved in the living organic system of the man, an imprint or archetype of all the ancestral experiences of the female, a deposit, as it were, of all the impressions ever made by woman. . . . Since this image is unconscious it is always unconsciously projected upon the person of the beloved, and is one of the chief reasons for passionate attraction or aversion."[8]

"In mythology, fairy tales, folklore, and poetry, we find strange beings like nymphs, swan maidens and fairies. As a rule, they are of enticing beauty but are only half human; they have fish tails, like the nixie, or turn into birds, like the swan maidens. . . . With charms and/or enchanting songs these beings (sirens, The Lorelei, and so on) lure a man into their realm, where he disappears forevermore; or else a very important point—they try to bind the man in love, that they may live in his world with him. Always they have something uncanny about them and there is a taboo connected with them that must not be broken."[9]

Jung believed the most essential aspects of a man's anima are openness and receptiveness, which are essential for human relationships and creativity. Most men are overly reasonable, overly directed, overly focused. They disdain feeling, intuition, and the irrational, and these aspects are then repressed. However, the anima figure representing all these characteristics serves to balance and compensate. If this aspect of a man is repressed, it makes its appearance in the form of a projection. In spite of his reasonable nature, his "head is turned" and he is overwhelmed by his unconscious as he projects it onto a woman.

Men's favored female entertainers are anima figures. Talent and ability do not play a major role in their choices, and intelligence does not seem to be a very important factor. The anima "captures" a man with her beauty, charm, and openness. Some answers to our questionnaire illustrate this:

"Barbara Bach is my favorite actress because she has an incredibly good-looking body—drool." (M, 20)

"Cybill Shepherd is the most beautiful thing I have ever seen in my entire life. She plays the roles of very quiet and timid girls which totally makes me go wild. She is one 'hell of a girl.' " (M, 21)

"Olivia Newton-John seems to touch the soft things in life. She captures me and her audience with her tender voice. Some of the songs she sings display a sexy and seductive atmosphere." (M, 19)

A few of the men we sampled had somewhat less primitive anima projections. Said one: "I've always had a crush on Carly

Simon. First of all, there is her physical appearance. She has beautiful long hair, full lips, high cheekbones, and a very sexy body. She is soft, graceful, but not weak or shy. She writes her own songs which are pretty good and plays the guitar well. She is not too tough but also seems independent and very together. I think she understands men and relationships between men and women." (M, 38)

Another responded, "Judy Collins is smooth, graceful, and beautiful. She is feminine but powerful and intelligent. She is sensitive and emotional." (M, 34)

Moving Targets

Because we sometimes lose interest in an entertainer or a celebrity doesn't mean that the projections disappear. Usually we take the projected image, almost intact, and find another entertainer who will carry it. As we grow and develop, the new target is more sophisticated and complete. Most celebrities realize this and try to get as much money as they can while they are a sensation (a target for archetypal projections) and before new heroes or dream lovers are found.

The intense illusions of the fan can only last for a limited time. We differ according to the speed with which we change targets. People who change slowly are characterized positively as loyal or "diehard" fans and negatively as old-fashioned. Fans who withdraw projections quickly and find new targets are thought to be either in fashion or fickle.

Developing our own heroic or masculine or feminine potential is clearly not easy. So often our projections persist, no matter how many times we have been disappointed. We see a favorite entertainer in an interview on TV or read what one has to say about some political issue and we become disillusioned. Then we find some new hero or dream lover to take that one's place.

One woman we interviewed spends her professional life interviewing celebrities. She was born on the East Coast and moved to Hollywood in order to have easier access to the stars. "When I began working, you can't imagine how thrilled I was to be meeting celebrities. I thought this was the greatest job in the world. But every single time I interviewed a star, my excitement turned to disappointment. They are really mostly a bunch of jerks. Now if there is a performer or singer I really admire, I won't do an interview. I don't want to find out he's a creep." Here is the unusual case of someone who has access to the targets of her projections. She meets and gets behind her own projections, and she finds herself constantly disappointed. Yet she continues to project. No wonder then that most of us who do not have her opportunity continue to project, although at times we must change targets.

Who Are the Fans?

When we began doing research for this chapter, we kept asking the experts: what kind of people are fans? How old, what sex? Are they unmarried or alone? Certainly there must be people who admire a person's acting or singing ability strictly because of his or her talent and technique, people who have reasonable, objective reactions to entertainers rather than strong emotional attachments. Such people we thought could be labeled admirers rather than fans, because objective admiration may not involve projection.

Is everybody a fan? Many people are involved with entertainers for a significant portion of their lives. Americans spend an average of five hours a day watching television, and one recent study of fifteen thousand children found that half would rather give up their fathers than give up their TVs.[10] Some people can't get enough or know enough about their favorite performers. Not only fan magazines but sports and women's magazines have celebrities on their covers. Pictures of celebrities sell these magazines, and they are getting more involved in selling other products as well. When we project mythical images, we transform the ordinary into the extraordinary. It is good sales strategy to link the extraordinary with a product you want to sell. Advertisers are of course aware of this phenomenon.

One movie critic said, "We are interested in entertainers because in them, we see something special, and people all need something special in their lives." What we see in them is quite special—the projected archetypes of the hero and dream lover—images that "impress, influence and fascinate" us, as Jung said. The more we asked the question "Who is the fan? the more it appeared that the answer is—everyone. James Seymour of *People* magazine said, "I've thought about this quite a lot and I think that everybody is a fan of some sort. Poets and philosophers develop cult followings." Some of us seem better able to control our behavior; we may seem unaffected when in fact we are very much "taken with" a celebrity. Although the targets vary depending on one's education, level of sophistication, style, and so forth, almost everyone is fascinated by a favorite entertainer.

One fan-magazine editor we spoke with contended that although there is a good deal of projection and fanaticism, she and many people she knew were not really fans. "I don't care about their personal lives," she said, "I appreciate them as professionals." As we left the restaurant where the interview took place, we passed a man with sunglasses accompanied by a strikingly attractive red-haired woman. The street was narrow, and they brushed passed us. "Did you see!" she said in a stifled cry. "That's Al Pacino. I wonder who he's with and where they are going."

The Target

Early in his career, Burt Reynolds parlayed his frequent appearances on "The Johnny Carson Show" into a veritable gold mine. They were instrumental in advancing his rise as a star. These guest shots worked because he appeared relaxed, amusing, disarmingly candid, and funny—attractive animus qualities in counterpoint to the "macho" buildup he had received in the press. Reynolds worked at being both a man's man (hero) and a woman's man (animus). What came across as nonchalance was actually the result of careful planning, of meticulous work on image—as Reynolds said, of paying attention to ". . . how to work the audience, how to use the camera, what to reveal and what to hold back, how to get hurt and come back, how to use the other guests."[11]

Although Reynolds has made it to the top, that kind of work on image has not stopped. He is not only maintaining his image, he is intelligently recasting it. In a prime-time nationwide interview with Barbara Walters, the actor appeared to be highly sensitive, vulnerable, and almost obsessed with a desire for a child. This appeared to be a new, interesting, and deepening aspect of Reynolds's personality, and people were very taken with it. What the audience did not know was that the actor was set to do a film called *Paternity*, all about a man who desperately wants a son.

Burt Reynolds is not alone in his ability to use the media. All stars use the media to help them become suitable targets. A good target image is one that activates the fans' projections. Although many stars are unaware of it, their fans are reacting to much more than the image Hollywood has created. Fans superimpose their own projections, which are much richer than the image, upon the

target. This is what accounts for the great emotional involvement
we feel with our favorite stars.

One critic spoke of the regular media route taken by most stars.
"First you want all the exposure, all the interviews and magazine
articles you can get. Then the minute you start getting exposure,
you become selective; then when you become really well known—
famous—you need to be elusive so that everybody is always dying
to hear about or see you." Another said, "Movie stars are the aris-
tocracy of entertainers. They try to maintain a real distance between themselves and their fans. This perpetuates the illusion
that they live interesting and mysterious lives. They come down
from the castle, make a movie, get phenomenal sums of money,
and then disappear into the glamorous Hollywood hills. Most big
stars realize that familiarity breeds contempt." Stars have to be
careful not to burst the bubble of projection.

The Suitable Target—Mystery and Money

As difficult as it is to attain star status, it is equally arduous to
maintain it. Since so much of what the public sees of stars is a
carefully constructed facade, distance is necessary to maintain
the illusion. From a distance, the image is a perfect target for
projection; from too close, the illusion dissolves.

There are different distancing devices used to keep the target
and thus the projections intact. One is created by the illusion that
the star is too removed, too special to really care about fan reaction—the distance created by the myth of self-sufficiency. To appear personally needy is not the stuff of heroes or dream lovers. Of
course, fans also need the targets to be close enough to touch at
times—the projections cannot extend light-years—so periodic
candor or show of slight human frailty helps maintain the image.
If we are occasionally allowed to peek through the cracks of the
image, it may enable us to think that all we see is real.

One of the greatest and most well known exploiters of mystery
as a path to stardom was Greta Garbo. When she first arrived in
America, she was reported to have been definite, honest, and open
with the press and others. She learned soon thereafter that there
was much more promise in being seen as "The Enigmatic Swede,"
"The Swedish Sphinx," and "The Mysterious Stranger." As it
happens, Garbo lived a life with many friends, parties, and lovers.
In his biography of her, Norman Zierold says that "If Garbo was
a hermit, she was surely the most gregarious hermit of her
time.... She has managed to live her own richly peopled life while

simultaneously retaining her mystique, assuring its survival long after her departure from films. The feat constitutes one of the bravura performances of our time."[12]

Gods and goddesses are in possession of awesome power. This power separates them from us by an unbridgeable chasm. In our society, money and power are equated. The fact that major entertainers get paid incomprehensible amounts endows them with an aura of power. If someone makes a couple of million dollars for a few months' work, they are definitely not like us. Their experience is removed from anything most people will ever know. This kind of distance helps set them up and maintain them as excellent targets for mythic projections.

Sometimes money itself is enough to create a good target. When Dave Winfield played for the San Diego Padres for a few hundred thousand dollars a year, he was simply an excellent all-around ball player. When he signed with the New York Yankees for $20 million, he didn't add one home run to his total or a point to his batting average, but he became a hero. We read as much about the money entertainers and athletes make as we do about their skills. We devour pictures of their castles, their fabulous jewels, their private jets and sumptuous parties. These are the proper trappings of the gods.

And of course their romances are part of their clear separation from us, too. A proper dream boy needs a dream girl, the hero, a heroine. The pairing of two celebrities makes a perfect spectacle for our projections.

Effects on the Target

According to professional interviewers, entertainment editors, managers, and the celebrities themselves, the majority of successful entertainers are quite able to distinguish themselves from their image. Although they don't use the psychological terms, their goal is to shape themselves in a way that will allow them to receive intense projections from their fans, and they know their business well. One movie critic said, "I think the stars are not fooled by these projections, as you call them. They need to be loved and admired by millions of people in order to get the best parts and make the most money and not vice versa. They strive for fame in order to make the really big money."

Psychotherapists understand the power and the dangers of being the target for projections. Jung said that in many therapy situations the client comes to see the analyst as a "savior." The projection of such a mythic image, if it happens often enough, can cause a therapist to believe that he is in fact a savior. Jung warned that repeated exposure to such projections can lead to a condition he called psychic inflation. Therapists have to be on guard against their patients' projections. No matter how tempting it is to believe that they are extraordinary creatures, they are not. If people confuse themselves with positive projections from others, they suffer psychic inflation—in more common terms, a swelled head.

If therapists must guard themselves against projections, imagine what celebrities must do! We are talking about millions of fans, millions of projections onto one person. It is difficult not to become confused, disoriented, overwhelmed by such an onslaught.

Not surprisingly, in general, the younger entertainers, the so-called teen idols, have the most difficulty handling projections. We were told by an entertainment editor that most of them had no idea that they were not their image. "They don't feel they are doing a job. They are really out of contact with the normal world. They are almost always controlled by some combination of their parents, their record or movie company, and public-relations people. Most are pretty successful in dealing with the pressure from fans because they are so young, with so much energy, and are too naive to know what is going on. By the time they hit twenty, most of them are finished. The career of the teen idol is by definition limited. Often when their 'reign' is over, they are completely baffled." Most of them believe they actually are the dream boys that their fans see. When you have little experience in life and thousands or millions of people see you as an extraordinary prince, you believe them. Since the idols' identity is so tied to their fans' projections, they are left with fragmented personalities when these projections dissolve. One reporter who covers these stars told us that "the crash that many teen stars take isn't seen or heard because it happens when they are out of sight—after we, the public, have lost all interest in them."

Age does not assure that a star will be able to judge the difference between reality and projection. Not all adult entertainers are equal to this task. As James Seymour pointed out, "When they seek fame, entertainers cannot possibly comprehend what they are getting into—they become separated from life. If they can't discriminate themselves from their fans' reactions, you get the stuff that Hollywood legends and tragedies are made from." The names of the legends go on—Jean Harlow, Marilyn Monroe, Jean

Seberg, Rudolph Valentino, John Gilbert, Elvis Presley, Freddie Prinze. There are conflicts, tensions, and severe burdens that result from being a target for mythic projections. All jobs come with pressures and stress, but job requirements seldom read: Needs the ability to cope with millions of archetypal projections. Fans do not see entertainers clearly, without projections, but neither do the entertainers themselves. It is this confusion about one's own identity caused by fan reaction that is so dangerous.

Profile of a Soap Star

For many reasons, it is difficult to find an entertainer who is willing to talk about projections. The usual line from entertainers is that although there are some fanatics, most fans don't believe that entertainers are heroes or dream lovers. Asking a performer if he wants to be seen as a mythical image and works to maintain such illusions is like asking a politician if he is interested in obtaining power. Politicians say their only interest is to serve the people, and entertainers say they only want to do good work.

Entertainment editors told us that a star's career is based on image, and they have to know exactly what would appear in print and how it would affect their image before they consent to do an interview. Celebrities grant interviews in a very calculated fashion—to hype new movies, or records, or to recast or maintain images. Most do not trust psychologists and believe that having interviews with them is not safe. We did speak with several entertainers, but only one was willing to talk to us with surprising candor—Denny Albee, a leading man on "One Life To Live," a daytime soap opera.

To 20 to 40 million soap-opera fans, Denny is Dr. Peter Jensen, all-American good guy. For five years, they have been watching him fight for justice, save lives, and get involved in very complex romantic relationships. In real life, Denny got a master's degree and taught school for a while in the Midwest before going into acting. His career was understandably aided by the fact that he is tall, with blond hair and blue eyes, and strikingly handsome.

The interview took place in the TV studio—one large floor of an old armory building—with about a dozen small sets, including bars, living rooms, bedrooms, restaurants, and several hospital rooms. Outside the studio were a dozen fans waiting for autographs and glimpses of their favorite stars! Inside, Dr. Peter Jensen was dying in one of the hospital rooms. It had been a difficult year for him: he was very much in love with one woman, while he was married to another; his wife had just been sent off to a mental hospital, and the woman he was in love with had just been married but had had her marriage annulled. She recently had had a baby from an altogether different man.

James Halpern: I'd like to know about your fans, what they are like and your reaction to them.

Denny Albee: The station screens our mail so we don't see the real perverse stuff. I get anywhere from a hundred to two hundred pieces of fan mail a month, maybe two to three thousand pieces a year. Some of it says they want to marry me, or they want their daughter to marry me. If you walk outside the theater, there are always a bunch of groupies.

We go out across the country and put on promotional shows in malls and arenas, and five to eight thousand people, mostly women, show up. Almost all the questions they ask are about your character. They can't disassociate the real person from the fantasy person.

J.H.: Who is the mail addressed to, you or Peter Jensen?

D.A.: There are a few people who write to say they think I'm doing a good job, but three quarters of my mail is to Peter. Most people in the street call me Peter. We are seen every day by people, so we are not treated like other stars. No one when they see Robert Redford calls out, "Hey, Sundance Kid!"

Of course those that don't watch daytime television don't know me from a hole in the wall, but the reaction of people who do watch is incredible. I can't shop at a supermarket or go into a shopping mall or department store. I'll be walking down an aisle and there will be two or three ladies following me around with their carts. "Look," one will say, "Dr. Peter Jensen bought Pledge, so let's get Pledge." They do this, they really do. It gets tiresome, especially if you're in a restaurant trying to eat.

J.H.: Does knowing what you know about fan reaction keep you from developing fantasies about other performers?

D.A.: I don't think you can get away from the star-fan relationship. What do I do for relaxation? I go to a movie or a play. Sammy Davis, Jr., comes on our show every year because he follows it. Even he had a glorified impression of us, of our characters on the soap.

I try not to develop emotional attachments to celebrities. I don't really call them stars; they are more people whom I admire. But I suppose I do idolize some people. As a matter of fact, I think I have emotional attachments to quite a few celebrities.

J.H.: How have your reactions to your fans' reactions changed over the years?

D.A.: At first, it was a large intrusion on my private life. When I walked out of the studio, I wanted to do whatever I wanted to do. When I get on planes, the airline stewardesses are hitting on me. Then I realized it comes with the territory. You have to keep it in perspective, you have to realize that you're not acting for yourself. There are no actors without fans. Many actors don't realize this. They are performing for an audience and turning out goods or products, and people love or hate or love to hate the character you're playing.

A woman from Philadelphia wrote me a letter about five years ago when I started doing soaps and said, "I love your character, could you please write me back." I took the time to write a two-page letter, and she wrote back to me saying, "You must not be very important." After that, I never wrote a fan back.

You can't burst their bubble; you have to be very careful not to destroy the image that you have prepared and worked for.

J.H.: Are you conscious of working at being a particular image as a target for fans to project on?

D.A.: Actually I would like to play a bad guy, that people love to hate. But my looks tend to keep me playing good-guy roles. You really can't go against character. I would probably be a lovable bad guy. You have to know what you can do in the business.

J.H.: How easy is it for you to tell the difference between who you are—Denny Albee—and how you are seen by your fans—Peter Jensen, M.D.?

D.A.: I don't know if I do disassociate and I don't know if I don't. That's tough because we do these characters all day long. There is a lot of me in the character and therefore a lot of the character in me. I'm not completely sure which came first. I am sure that I take a lot of my personality and put it into the character. We have to do this in the soaps because we do it so regularly. I've known people playing a totally different character than themselves, and it's really a strain. They have nervous breakdowns and bad relationships. Five minutes ago, I was Peter dying, and now I'm Denny. In a little while, I'll be Peter again and I have to be into the character enough to be believable to forty million people. It takes me a half-hour to get into it. I'll lay in that hospital bed for a half-hour getting into Peter. There are a lot of emotional problems in this business, especially for the people playing the villain. If they get slugged, they have to realize they're not the character, or "My God, what did I do?"

J.H.: Do you merit all the adulation that you get?

D.A.: Not really, no. But the character does. He's really a great guy, a great character. He deserves the attention. But Denny? Ha, I'm not that nice a guy, not that nice a person in all ways. But I go back and forth from Denny to Peter. I think the best actors in this business are schizo. We all hide behind the character we play. And I suppose a little bit of Peter is coming out in this interview. In business and other things, I'm not really such a nice guy. I think I enjoy being somebody I'm not. I think that's the reason I got into this business.

We're not allowed to be ourselves. I don't feel I'm allowed to be myself. When I walk into a store or restaurant, I'm not allowed to be Denny by the people around me. They want me to be Peter. They treat me like Peter. I know that now. I fought it for a long time, but now I use it. I say, "Could I get a little extra salad?" or "Could you warm the coffee up?" "What's really the best thing in the kitchen?"

J.H.: What effect does all this have on your real relationships? Not being able to separate what is projected on you and who you are must be difficult for your relationships outside the studio.

D.A.: Yes, it takes its effect, and that question hits pretty close to home. I was with the same woman for five years. Up until about six months ago, and we are separated now. It's mostly thanks to her strength and constitution that it went that long. It's very hard to do this kind of work and not drag it home. There are all these crises going on here, and it's hard not to take them home.

After my separation, I dated a girl who was a fan and I didn't know it. I didn't know she knew who I was in the business. Halfway through the evening, in a very intimate moment, she called me Peter. I was upset and angry. I have found out in the six months since I've been separated how difficult it is to develop a real relationship.

Since I've been separated, I've been trying to figure out my relationships with women. It's easy to find relationships as Peter, but ultimately that's not very satisfying to Denny.

I tell you why relationships are hard to maintain for people in this business. I've thought about this over the years. What are relationships, anyway? Basically relationships with people are emotional involvement, and this is precisely what I get paid for. I get paid to go up there on the set and show and display my emotional involvements—to have feelings, to cry, love, hate—all those things that make up normal relationships. I get paid for displaying these, and doing it right. This is why so many actors fall in love with their leading ladies and vice versa. We have thirty-one regular people on the show, and there are six real couples. Twelve out of the thirty-one are in couple relationships. These are people who dumped their wives or their husbands—that's a high percentage. When you lie there in bed saying you love each other twelve hours a day (over a year now with my leading lady), with ten or fifteen bedroom scenes, holding each other, kissing passionately, making love as the camera fades out—nobody is that good a liar.

We're being paid to display the passions of life, and then you go home, and it's kind of tough on your relationship, your wife. They understand that, they know it, but they don't understand what it's like in your heart. There are a lot of people who fall apart in this business, going back and forth from character to real person.

J.H.: What are your thoughts and feelings about the fact that so many people are involved in relationships based on illusion or projection? At one point over sixty million Americans were more involved with J.R. (from the TV show "Dallas") than they were with a real person.

D.A.: Our society is entertainment oriented—show me this, show me that. Everybody goes and sees everything, and we do less and less ourselves. I think people love to hate J.R. because something in their own life is not being fulfilled. People have a lot of time that they don't know what to do with.

A prime-time television series lasts maybe thirteen weeks, whereas we on the soaps are a constant. We're there for people every day. I think it's incredible that we are so much a part of people's lives. It must fulfill something in people because it can become as important to them as their own children or work. They want to see a great deal of emotional stuff messed around, and they love to see us in pain. We're modern gladiators. Rather than living their own lives, they project it all onto us and they live vicariously through us.

Profile of a Fan

Although projections are illusions, they have a tremendous impact on the lives of all entertainers. As fans, we all know that our favorite stars have an impact on our lives. For some, their presence is felt more keenly. In the following example, we see how it is possible to learn about what our favorite stars really mean to us and how we can understand ourselves through our projections onto them.

"I am totally in love with James Taylor," Georgia told us sincerely. "His music, even his appearance conveys to me the image of a sensitive and gentle man. I see him as sensitive because he exposes his vulnerability in his music. He readily admits to his frailties in songs but he doesn't get lost in life's horrors. Many of his songs express views that are cheery and optimistic. I dislike men that feign absolute emotional strength because it is so false. James Taylor doesn't do this, and it makes him seem more honest about who he is as a person as well as more honest with himself. His person comes out in his music.

"On the other hand, some of his songs are decidedly romantic and up. I guess I'm touched by a man that can write and sing about the wonder and magic of the sun. It is this gentle quality that I find most appealing.

"Most of my impressions which have grown into beliefs about him have come from my listening to his albums. I have never seen him in concert, although I have always wanted to.

"His appearance also has much to do with how I see him. When I was a very little girl, I loved to watch Bible stories on TV because I thought the men with long flowing hair and long soft beards were especially handsome compared to the crew cuts and clean-shaven faces of the day. I was delighted with the look of men of the sixties, needless to day. James Taylor fit that image when his first album came out—his long, thick, dark hair combined with strong features and soft earth-tone clothes.

"Really, I guess, he is everything I want in a man. I have never found anyone who comes close to him. Certainly not John, my ex. I was married very, very young—seventeen, in fact, and divorced at nineteen. I married to get away from my family, but marriage didn't give me what I was looking for.

"John (my husband) was a traditional type—into cars, sports—but I thought that he was also pretty gentle and warm. I was looking for someone to take care of me, be caring with me. I thought John would do it, but it didn't work out."

Just as listing the qualities that annoy us about someone can be very instructive, being specific about the attraction our favorite stars hold can also teach us a lot about our mythic projections. For Georgia, James Taylor is an excellent target for the projection of her animus figure.

What is it about him that she finds so appealing? Georgia's animus captures her through the power of the word—his poetry. In it, she finds the combination of strength and sensitivity, nurturance and masculinity that are lacking in her conscious life. Taylor is in touch with his emotions but not overwhelmed by them. His success makes him a figure of power and strength. From Georgia's description of her early marriage, it is clear that she projected these animus qualities onto her husband. However, he was unable to hold the projection for very long. Georgia has been a fan of Taylor's for many years; he has been a much more successful target for her projections. Doing a bit of analysis of what we really like about our favorite stars will often produce a good description of our hero or our dream lover. It's a good way for us to become acquainted with the mythic figures of our unconscious.

8

Politics and the News

According to *The New York Times,* "Local newscasts are looking more and more like entertainment series these days. What's happening is simple enough: News has become a hit, the largest source of revenue for many local stations. . . . Recently stations have discovered that news—particularly when it's presented in a jazzy dramatic fashion—can be more entertaining than reruns. . . ."[1]

If you are unfortunate enough to wake up to a local radio news station in a large American city, you are likely to know within minutes if anyone was murdered in a taxi or a subway, if anyone threw a brick from a roof in downtown, if there are any recent developments in the murder trials of famous victims. The more bizarre, it seems, the better. Local television newscasts are expanding, with more coverage of child pornography, child prostitution, and other topics that sadden, anger, and disappoint their viewers. Yet people are fascinated by these stories. They say, "It is horrible," but they remain transfixed by the radio or television. It is clear that these stories get so much air time because people are entertained by them.

Why are people fascinated by these horror stories? What holds them while they feel repelled? The force of our projection of the shadow draws us to stories of villains and violence. The graphic way that the media present these stories facilitates these projections. The media present great targets for us.

Many Americans have become geared to receiving all their information about current events, including politics, through the broadcast media. And the presentation of political events is moving quickly in the direction of an entertainment spectacle. The differences among entertainment, the news, and politics are becoming less and less distinct. Entertainers are becoming politicians, politicians become news anchors, and so on.

It makes sense that politics and other world events can easily become entertainment. Beyond our intellectual interest in politics and other world events, we have an interest in and fascination with political figures because they are good targets for the projection of two basic and important mythic images—the hero and the shadow. We are entertained, therefore, because our interest is powerfully engaged through projection.

The Watergate hearings, for example, were not only significant political events but high drama and fabulous entertainment. For millions of Americans, Nixon was an important target for projections. Many saw him as an embattled hero, while for many others, he was a target for their unconscious desires to manipulate and control. They projected all their unsavory characteristics onto him, and he held the projections well. When Nixon was forced out of office, many conservatives missed him, but he was probably missed most by those who hated him. They had to find a new target for their shadow projections.

It seemed to us that the people who program the news would be most aware of this phenomenon. Their job is to attract viewers, to entertain people, so they must know what a "good" story is. If an archvillain or a knight in shining armor appears, a good news person should recognize that this means a good hook is available for our projections.

We contacted NBC News to ask about the relationship between entertainment, news, and politics. We also wanted to know if network officials were conscious of the power of mythic images such as the hero and shadow and our need to project them. We were somewhat startled by the extreme point of view that the NBC news official took.

NBC Person: I've heard some strange ideas before, but this one doesn't even come out of left field. It comes from out past the bleachers somewhere. We report the news; we report what happens and what is happening in the world.

Us: But you are also concerned about what is interesting to your viewers. If your viewers are fascinated by certain kinds of stories—say, somebody who mysteriously rescues people in distress—rather than the actions of the city council—you'll report the story your viewers want to see.

NBC: No. We report what's going on—take it or leave it—that is our attitude. The news is inflation, Poland under martial law, the current cold wave. There are no mythical heroes or anti-heroes in all this.

Us: Of course we are not saying that all news involves projection. But how else do you explain people's fascination with Patty Hearst, or the Forty-four Caliber Killer, or the Jean Harris murder trial? Aren't these events dramatic, and if so, what makes them dramatic—why are people so captivated by certain stories? We don't think projection plays a part in people's interest in the cold snap, but there are other stories where maybe it does play a part.

NBC: You seem to be saying that we present the news to entertain people, and we don't. If you take out station breaks and commercials, we have twenty-two minutes to tell people what is happening. We don't have time to entertain them. To prove my point, I'll send you the transcripts of our news shows for the last few months. You can examine them.

A recent report from *Time* magazine concluded that what people want most from the news is entertainment and diversion.[2] Could the network spokesman be right in asserting that they were not interested in entertaining its viewers? It is difficult to say with certainty; the promised transcripts never arrived.

The Cause of Evil: The Shadow

What is the source of all the aggression and conflict in the world? Biologists and behavioral scientists have posited many causes: aggressive behavior is learned, or imitated, or it is caused by frustration; or it has a strong inborn or genetic component. Konrad Lorenz has argued that humans have been successful in the evolutionary struggle because of our powerful innate tendencies to aggress.[3] Freud took this position and felt, therefore, that the source of evil and aggression in the world may well be within us all.

The element of truth behind all this which people are so ready to disavow, is that men are not gentle creatures who want to be loved, and who at the most can only defend themselves if they are attacked; they are, on the contrary, creatures among whose instinctual endowment is to be reckoned a powerful share of aggressiveness. As a result, their neighbor is for them not only a potential helper or sexual object, but also someone who tempts them to satisfy their aggressiveness on him, to exploit his capacity for work without compensation, to use him sexually without his consent, to seize his possessions, to humiliate him, to cause him pain, to torture and to kill him. *Homo homini lupus* (man is wolf to man).[4]

According to Freud, each of us learns to stifle his anger in the interests of society and to direct the anger back toward himself. The effects of this unconscious process are felt as guilt. Thus, in order to live in society, each person exchanges a portion of happiness for a portion of security and the inevitable accompaniment of guilt. This is Freud's explanation for why everyone feels vaguely unhappy or discontent; our aggression, instead of being directed at others, is focused back on ourselves.

If aggression is directed outward indiscriminately, there is chaos; if it is not directed outward at all, there is guilt and unhappiness. But there is another alternative.

If we get angry or act destructively, we can believe it is always in response to someone else's anger or aggression. This reactive stance—I'm only being nasty in response to the other guy—helps to protect us from our own evil. We are able to accomplish this psychological protection by projecting our shadow onto someone else. Jung agreed with this point of view. In 1937, he wrote, "Unfortunately there can be no doubt that man is on the whole less good than he imagines himself or wants to be. Everyone carries a shadow and the less it is embodied in the individual's conscious life, the blacker and denser it is."[5]

An individual projects his shadow onto another because to see evil within creates disharmony for that individual. He can blame another for his unhappiness, be distracted from his own negative qualities, strike out against the other and thus express and release his own evil side, feeling self-righteous about destroying the other.

The same process, with all the benefits and dangers, can operate on a collective as well as an individual basis. As a group, we can project aggression on particular members of the group or on another group. This keeps everyone happy with themselves and each other. As Freud explained: "It is always possible to bind together a considerable number of people in love so long as there are other people left over to receive the manifestations of their aggressiveness. . . . When once the Apostle Paul had posited universal love between man as the foundation of his Christian community, ex-

treme intolerance on the part of Christiandom towards those who
remained outside became the inevitable consequence."[6]

Shadows in the News

This, then, is an explanation for our deep interest in the constant barrage of newscasts containing criminal, aggressive, and
brutal content. We need these newscasts, because they provide
convenient receptacles for the projection of our shadow. We
awake each morning to the news or morning paper and find out
that we are not criminals, that we are not brutal, selfish, and destructive, but that someone else is. We experience revulsion,
anger, the desire to bring back capital punishment and begin the
day having externalized our shadow. After a day at work, feeling
frustrated and angered, we watch the evening news and go to
sleep having exorcised all our demons.

A "good story" involving violence requires a suitable target. A
single act of aggression, whether it is planned or occurring at
random, does not provide the same drama or proper hook for our
projections as the work of some mysterious demonic figure. The
news media provide catchy names for deranged killers—"The
Boston Strangler," "The 44-Caliber Killer," "Son of Sam," "The
Slasher," "The Tylenol Killer." These hooks, shaped by the news
media, are designed to capture a large audience; the lure is the
suitable target for shadow projections. Certainly, as in all relationships, there is more than projection operating. We are concerned and frightened by mad killers; but our reactions go beyond
concern to fascination. When deranged killers are no longer selling newspapers and news shows, they sell books and movies. People want to know everything about their projected shadows.

The targets for our shadow projections come in many different
sizes and shapes, so that each of us can find a hook most suitable to
our own style. The psychotic murderer is only one possibility. The
archetype represents all that is inferior, immoral, self-serving,
and brutal. People on "the right" can project these qualities onto
welfare recipients (seen as lazy and manipulative), feminists
(seen as killing unborn infants), liberals (seen as stealing hard-
earned money through taxation), and foreigners (seen as bent on
the destruction of the United States). Those on "the left" can also
have distorted perceptions and see similar qualities in different
groups. There are the businessmen (seen as engaging in unscru-
pulous practices and cheating the government), the police (seen

as brutalizing the poor), the military (seen as bent on destroying the world), and the "rich" (seen as stealing, deceiving, and manipulating everyone).

Shadows in Prejudice and Politics

The phenomenon of anti-Semitism is an excellent example of shadow projection at its most intense. Over the centuries, Jews have been a small, identifiable population, different enough from the mainstream to be excellent targets for projection of the shadow. In 1950, T. W. Adorno and others, in their book *The Authoritarian Personality*, offered scientific support for the notion that projection plays a major role in anti-Semitism. The researchers studied over two thousand Americans and found that anti-Semites had unusually high evaluations of themselves, their parents, and their country. "We are just terrific. Our moms and dads were about as close to perfection as you can get and the American system is close to the ideal." Anti-Semites are thus a pretty upbeat group. Unless you are a member of a minority group, they are probably a lot of fun to be with. Unfortunately, they see Jews and other minorities as possessing all the negative and unsavory qualities they refuse to see in themselves.[7]

These findings are consistent with Jung's suggestions that the less we are conscious of our own shadow, the denser it becomes. If we are blind to our own capacity for evil, we project it outward and self-righteously condemn the Jews, the blacks, or whoever is the most appropriate scapegoat. When we deny the shadow within, evil takes us over.

Jews have been such a popular target for the projection of the shadow that they don't even have to be present to receive the projections. Recently, as the Solidarity Movement was gaining momentum in Poland, the government there engineered an anti-Semitic campaign. A wall poster in Warsaw proclaimed that Lech Walesa, a devout Roman Catholic and union leader, was actually a Jew, as were other prominent Solidarity leaders. The Polish government, under attack itself, was hoping to divert some hostility from itself onto the Jews. What was most astonishing about the episode is that in the aftermath of the Holocaust, there are virtually no Jews left in Poland. In fact, "most Poles under the age of 30 have never met a Jew."[8]

Hitler could certainly be considered an expert on the use of anti-Semitism to further political goals. He was reported to have said that "anti-Semitic propaganda in all countries is an almost indispensable medium for the extension of our political campaign. You will see how little time we shall need to upset the ideas and criteria of the whole world simply and purely by attacking Judaism."[9]

Hitler was then asked if the Jews should be destroyed, to which he replied, "No . . . we should then have to invent him. It is necessary to have a tangible enemy, not merely an abstract one."[10]

Anti-Semitism is an unusual example of shadow projection because through it, one group has served as the target for many different groups of people. Usually the targets change with the time and the place. "The enemy" of a nation usually changes through time. And "the enemy" is the target for the shadow projection.

It is useful for the internal political stability of a nation to have enemies, whether they are real or imaginary. Aristotle argued that the internal stabilty of a country can be most threatened when there are no external enemies. He said that politicians sometimes need to "foster alarms" in order to put men at their guard.[11] As long as the shadow is projected outward, as long as another nation is hated and feared, our personal concerns and internal problems take a backseat.

In the individual, there is a direct relationship between the force of the negative, shadow side being denied and the strength of the shadow being projected. The same is true for a group or even a whole nation.

In Nazi Germany, Hitler came to power *not* by glorifying war or conquest but by advocating peace, by advocating respect for the rights of others, by advocating conventional morality, and by advocating truthfulness. In his words and perhaps in some sense in his thoughts also, he and Germany were *morally spotless*. An example of this is seen in a speech Hitler gave in 1939, in which he said:

I wish to point out first, that I have not conducted any war; second, that for years past I have expressed my abhorrence of war and, it is true, also my abhorrence of warmongers; and third, that I am not aware for what purpose I should wage a war at all.[12]

While Hitler was convincing the German people and perhaps himself of their own self-righteousness and morally superior position, he was also emphasizing the demonic nature of Germany's enemy. War against Czechoslovakia was declared because, as he told the Reichstag in 1939, that country was:

> ... a bridge to Europe for Bolshevik aggression, and to act as the mercenary of European democracies against Germany. What was expected from this state is shown most clearly by the observation of the French Air Minister, M. Pierre Cot, who calmly stated that the duty of this state in case of any conflict was to be an airdome for the landing and taking off of bombers from which it would be possible to destroy the most important German industrial centers in a few hours.[13]

His attack on Poland was justified, he told the same body later that year, because of "the sudden Polish general mobilization, followed by more atrocities. ... I have therefore resolved to speak to Poland in the same language that Poland for months has used toward us."[14]

What makes these examples striking to us is that someone who has been so identified with evil was successfully able to present himself as a moral and peace-loving leader and to convince a nation that evil existed only in neighboring nations. It is unusual for any nation to perceive itself as the aggressor. Evil is almost always projected. When the Soviet Union invaded Afghanistan, it was done "to maintain a stable and friendly government and to stop the U.S. and other outside interferences." Similarly, United States officials maintained that our involvement in Vietnam was intended to "stop an invading enemy." No one accepts blame for war; evil exists only in someone else or in another nation. Nations all respond aggressively to their neighbor's aggression.

We are not saying that it is the projection of the shadow that causes war but rather that the projection of this archetype plays a powerful psychological role in the development of conflict and the willingness of people to enter combat.

If we examine the news stories and political events that have captivated the public recently, we can usually find a large component of projection in the involvement with the event. The "Iranian hostage crisis" comes to mind as one in which there were clearly a number of kinds of projection at work.

We knew little about the hostages themselves, but we identified with them, undoubtedly exaggerating their similarity to us. The Iranian captors and, more than anyone, the Ayatollah (a hero in his own country), held our shadow projection. For Americans, the event was much more than a political struggle; many people felt

America was being held by the forces of evil. The Iranians, of
course, also projected their shadows onto the United States. We
saw crowds of thousands chanting "Death to the American satan"
and "Cut off the hands of the infidel Carter." Because the Iranian
culture is alien to our own, the captors were excellent hooks for
the projection of the unknown shadow.

The conflict between the United States and Iran represented
our own personal inner conflicts. Westerners have modern conve-
niences, have made scientific and technological advances, and do
things more quickly. We have paid a price, however, because by
moving so quickly forward in one direction, we have left behind
our emotions and those aspects of ourselves that are timeless. No
wonder we were so frightened by the Muslim fundamentalists and
their hold to the past. They viewed the conflict as primarily a spir-
itual and religious one. Their intensity and their emotionality,
expressed in their chants and their willingness to die, were frightening to us. Onto the Ayatollah and the Iranians, we projected
the alien parts of ourselves. We who pride ourselves on our ration-
ality do not see that it is developed at the expense of our feeling
lives. "Nuke Iran" was the cry to destroy the feared emotional aspects of ourselves.

The Iranian crisis became a national obsession. Night after
night for over fourteen months, the entire nation agonized over
the fate of fifty-two hostages. Every day Americans were dying or
killing each other in accidents or on purpose, but we paid no attention. In Iran, we were captured by our unknown selves—by
our projections—and this process was aided greatly by both the
news media and the politicians.

George Ball, one-time adviser to President Carter and undersec-
retary of state, recalled that over eighty-three crew members from
the ship *Pueblo* were held for over a year by the North Koreans;
some were even tortured. And yet it was not made into a major
news event because television could not cover it. Bell said that in
Iran, "Television played it like a soap opera and made it the greatest soap opera of the year. . . . Television played the situation up
so that it has become the central issue of American policy, which
is absurd."[15]

Television is not solely to blame for the exaggerated reactions of
the American people. A producer of a major news network indicated that if the government had had nothing to say about the
hostage crisis, there would not have been one. According to him,
the Carter administration had something to gain by playing up

the situation. In terms of projection, the benefits to the administration of the crisis are clear. Carter was involved in a bitter fight for renomination; he asked Americans to rally around him in his struggle against the devils from Iran, and they did. The administration and the news cooperated—or colluded—in achieving an American obsession with the hostage situation, which contributed to Carter's renomination. As months passed, however, Carter became the victim of his own strategy; he was unable to play the heroic role of actually bringing the hostages home, and a new hero was sought.

The Hero in Politics and the News

We met the hero in our discussion of stars and fans. But now that you are well acquainted with the shadow, the hero's role in our psyche should be clearer. Just as the villain, the hated minority group, and the office scapegoat represent a projection of our shadow archetype, the hero represents our gallant and positive side—our desire to overcome the immature or negative aspects within us. National leaders, politicians, and other public figures are common targets for this mythic projection.

Joseph Campbell's book *The Hero with a Thousand Faces* demonstrates that the basic qualities of the hero have remained the same across time and culture.[16] His work supports Jung's theory that the ability to produce the formal image of the hero is inborn. The various myths and legends of the hero all symbolize the drive and the struggle for self-realization.

The myth begins with the hero being called to adventure. If this call is not heeded, the hero will be ruined. Often, the hero who turns from the summons is cast into a spell. On the psychological level, this means that at some point in our lives, we recognize the importance of being true to our own feelings and thoughts. We must break with convention and strike out on our own. If we do not have the courage to do this, we will stagnate, symbolized in myths as being cast into a spell.

The hero's first encounter is often with a protective older figure who provides some advice or protective device for use against danger. The hero then crosses the first threshold—the border between the safe and the dangerous. Beyond this threshold lies peril, that is, the dangerous elements of the unconscious symbolized by deserts, deep seas, jungles, alien lands, huge forests, and the like. Once the hero is in the unknown region, a succession of trials and tribulations are faced. Often the hero meets the temptations of sexuality, atones with the father image, and meets the beautiful goddess or princess. As the hero encounters and interacts with each of these forces, he is transformed. The contradictory aspects of his own nature meet and unite. The hero, after appearing to die, is reborn and transformed into an androgynous figure who is also at one with the protecting father. When the hero's quest has been accomplished, he returns to the world and is capable of helping and assisting those around him.

The hero myth represents the human drive for growth and self-realization. We are always terrified of being overwhelmed by our primitive, instinctual, aggressive nature. The forces of cooperation and love struggle to gain control over these negative forces. The psychological transformation that comes when we are able to fully realize both the heroic and shadow qualities within is symbolized by the prize (often gold) that the hero attempts to wrest through his fight with the enemy. When we see someone as a heroic figure, all these unconscious contents are part of what we are projecting.

For most of us, the call to adventure comes in our adolescence, when we attempt to break with convention, often taking risks that place us in danger. The quest is expressed in many different forms: fights for idealistic causes, going to war, dedication to a sport or profession or creative activity. Often the heroic quest of the adolescent is expressed in a less socially acceptable form: running away from home, driving cars extremely fast, taking drugs, or committing a crime. These can all be expressions of the desire to follow the quest for adventure and transformation.

Even when the desire is expressed in a socially useful form, for most of us, the heroic quest is short-lived. It is a difficult path, and the exigencies of life often demand that we abandon it. As adults, we speak of the great adventures of youth. However, the heroic quest continues to have great psychological significance. Although our heroic impulses are forced underground, they find expression in our projections. Many of us find our targets for this mythic projection in public figures. A good leader is one who can appear to encompass the aspects of the hero myth that most of us have not fully developed in ourselves. Someone who attracts such projections is said to have charisma.

Two political scientists, Dan Nimmo and James Combs, argue in their recent book *Subliminal Politics* that the same basic myth of the hero who saves the people from evil underlies *all* American politics.[17]

Our Heroic Past

We do not actually have to see the target for our hero archetype in order to project this mythic image. In fact, many of the most common and powerful targets are past heroes. Americans have tolerated all sorts of difficulties in the present—corrupt officials, lost wars, economic hardship—because we project the impersonal or collective image of the hero onto America's past leaders and have the hope that a country built by magical, magnificent leaders will soon be led to salvation by a new hero, who will vanquish all our foes.

Myths of a nation's past heroes are used to bolster the legitimacy of a current regime. In the Soviet Union, for example, Marx and Lenin are seen beyond their position as politicians or scholars and are granted superhuman powers. The current regime attempts to perpetuate its authority by linking itself to a superhuman heroic past, just as authority in royalty and some religious systems is maintained by legacy. The legends of a heroic past help us maintain our projections of power on our current leaders.

Nations value *foundation myths.* No matter how badly things are going today, we can take comfort in the past. We know the nation can right itself because the foundation was built by heroes and supermen.

A central figure in America's foundation myth is George Washington. In 1981, we asked 100 college students to name the past American politician they most admired or respected; Washington finished second. Mason Locke Weems, Washington's biographer, has been called the father of the father of his country. In the fifth edition of Weems's book, he told the tale familiar to all Americans—of Washington and the cherry tree. "I cannot tell a lie, Pa; you know I cannot tell a lie. I did it with my hatchet." This story appeared for the first time long after Washington's death. Nicholas Cords and Patrick Gerster, in their book *Myth in American History,* describe many such heroic deeds which probably never happened and yet have become part of our history.[18]

Teaching the myth of our heroic past is a very important aspect of the socialization process. Although we may be at each other's throats, we believe we share a common history of greatness. The fact that we share heroes—that we have common targets for our projections—holds us together as a group in the same way that sharing a common scapegoat can unite us.

In our poll of college students, John F. Kennedy, Jr., emerged as the greatest American hero by a landslide. Most political heroes attempt to claim humble origins. It helps us maintain hero projections if we think someone struggled to power from humble beginnings. Kennedy was clearly unable to do this, and yet more than anyone, he has successfully contained the hero projections of Americans. Other aspects of his life and personality made him an excellent target. He fought in World War II. His youthful and vigorous leadership called for personal sacrifice. His "New Frontier" evoked images of America's heroic past. He confronted the steel companies and forced them not to raise prices and confronted the Soviet Union and forced them to stop bringing missiles into Cuba. With these actions, Kennedy fought the shadow and won. The Kennedy image was also aided by a glamorous wife and two adorable children who were photographed often at the White House and on the beaches of Hyannis.

In our chapter 7, Stars and Fans, it was mentioned that the projector and the target should not be separated by light-years. Kennedy, a man with a background of so much wealth and privilege, became a better heroic target because of his self-deprecating humor. It made him seem more accessible and "human." When Kennedy was asked about how he got to be a war hero, he replied, "It was involuntary—they sank my boat."

Most of us don't have to be concerned about being perceived as too perfect. Social psychologists have found that if someone who is perceived as mediocre commits a blunder, he or she is seen as less attractive. However, it has also been shown that someone who is perceived as almost perfect becomes more attractive if he or she makes a mistake.[19] This is what accounts for the amazing fact that Kennedy's popularity rating rose and was never higher than right after the failed Bay of Pigs invasion.

The results of his decision to invade Cuba suggested to Americans that their hero was mortal. But what has virtually guaranteed his heroic stature is his tragic death. It is easiest to project the hero image on someone who is not living, since that person can no longer disappoint us. When someone dies, we can reconstruct the past, reinterpret actions and events, and find the most suitable hook for our projection. It was only after Kennedy's death that the entire story and mythology surrounding the Kennedys unfolded. Jacqueline Kennedy told how the President loved the musical *Camelot,* and how as a sickly child, he loved to read about King Arthur and the Knights of the Round Table. Mrs. Kennedy said that for Jack, history was full of "shining heroes."

Kennedy's legend lives on, although at the time that he died, his popularity rating had been declining to its lowest level. In recent years, when presidents enter office, their popularity ratings are in the 80 to 90 percent range. As they begin to make policy and decisions, they are seen as being responsible for bad conditions; their popularity falls. If any of our recent presidents—Truman, Eisenhower, Nixon, Ford, Carter, Reagan—had been killed in their first year of office, the initial projections of the hero would have stayed intact and any one of them would now be remembered as a great president.

Today there are many people who believe that the country would be a vastly different place if Kennedy had lived. Although he supported our involvement in Vietnam, people believe he would have terminated that involvement. Many also suggest there would be less corruption, less cynicism, less racism, and more idealism. If only Kennedy had lived, they believe, the turmoil and difficulties of the sixties and seventies would have been avoided.

Political Heroes Today

A good politician has to have, then, an intuitive understanding of psychology and the process of projection. Almost all political speeches sound as though the speaker recognizes the importance of manipulating the audience's parallel, shadow, and hero projections. Here is a hypothetical speech similar to many that we have heard, viewed in terms of projection.

Parallel projection. First the speaker establishes a sense of security and nonthreatening similarity between himself and the audience.

My wife, two children, and myself are always glad to be here in Dubuque. It reminds me so much of my own home town—a simple place where people understand the importance of basic things—family, hard work, the land, decency, and respect. Dubuque High School, which won the state championship, tells us a lot about what is needed to keep America strong and healthy. I played football in high school and I learned there that hard work, cooperation, discipline, intelligence, and strength are what are needed for a person, a team, and a nation to be successful.

Shadow projections. Next the speaker provides a receptacle for the audience's shadow projections. By attacking certain targets, everyone finds release for frustration and anger.

America today is a great nation—we are a proud people—
but we are threatened from within and without our country.
Although we are rich enough to take care of the truly needy,
we must ferret out the welfare cheats who distort and pervert
the system. Why, one woman in New York City [if speech is
given in New York, substitute Los Angeles] received over
$10,000 for welfare while she was in prison. It is this kind of
waste that is draining our energy. But it is not only these
"free riders" that are bilking the public. There are a number
of corporate executives who place their own interests and
profits above the good of the nation and stop at nothing in
their pursuit of greed. These white-collar criminals give business a bad name and force hardworking Americans to subsi-
dize their crimes. Criminals in our society—some rich, some
poor— must be dealt with quickly, firmly, justly.

On other occasions, I have spoken out about the threat im-
posed by [some other nation]. Every year they increase their
defense spending by twice the amount we do. Although we
are the mightiest nation on this earth, we must not be lulled
into a sense of false security. Our nation is threatened, and
we must continue to be vigilant and prepared militarily.

Hero projections. Now the speaker demonstrates that he can
successfully do battle with the forces of evil and restore the nation, conceived in greatness, to glory.

We can have a country where people who want work can
get it, where the disadvantaged can be helped, and where its
people have no doubts about its strength to remain at peace.
For most of my adult life—in business, in sports, as an astro-
naut, in Congress—I have found that the battle that must be
fought is against waste and lethargy. We can take care of the
poor and build our defense simultaneously. What *must* be sacrificed is waste. The unnecessary bureaucrats, the welfare
cheats, the padded military expenditures must and will be
rooted out in my administration. This is what my administration pledges to you today.

Washington, Lincoln, and Kennedy did not sacrifice
strength for compassion or compassion for strength. We must
not, cannot choose one of two necessities. These great presidents are remembered because each in his own way refused to
surrender to weakness or heartlessness. This is the tradition I
will restore, with your help on election day. Thank you.

This was obviously not a great political speech, but it is similar to many we have heard and are likely to hear in elections to come. It is designed to manipulate the kinds of projections common in politics.

If an aspiring presidential candidate says that our society is so complex that it is naive to think that one man can control the direction of the country, he will not be elected. If he honestly acknowledges all his doubts or weaknesses, he will not be elected. We demand that our politicians accept our projections of the hero.

In *The Selling of the President,* Joe McGinniss presented a behind-the-scenes account of Richard Nixon's campaign for the presidency in 1968, showing how advisers carefully crafted the image that would be presented to the American people. Nixon's staff created a suitable target for people to project onto. "This is the beginning of a whole new concept," said one of Nixon's advisers. "This is the way they'll be elected forevermore. The next guys up will have to be performers."[20]

Jeff Greenfield, former political speech writer and media consultant, noted that politics has always been involved with myth and symbolism. In the 1840 presidential election, William Harrison, who came from an affluent family, began the famous American tradition of suggesting that he began life in a log cabin. Greenfield's position is that "We have had plumed knights, and happy warriors and giant killers for as long as we have had campaigns."[21]

Now more than ever, because of the dominant position of television, physical appearance—how much a person looks like a good target—is crucial. This is the field where battles are lost and won.

... politics is already heavily influenced by television's Q rating system, which determines whether a performer gets the job. A Q rating (The "Q" stands for quotient) is a specific calculation of a performer's public appeal, with weight being given to the familiarity (or viewer recognition) factor, and, particularly, the strength of the favorable response to his name and face: likeability, or—since sexiness counts— lovability. ... Polls and Q ratings are fast becoming the political "p's" and "q's" that candidates must keep on eye on.[22]

In our search for the hero who will put America back on track, we seem to be directing our attention more and more to actors, sports figures, or astronauts who may look the part. Even politicians sometimes have difficulty distinguishing actors from themselves. William Buckley suggested that Dan Duryea "would make a fine director of the F.B.I." He was probably thinking about John Duryea, the politician, but his remark seems to "endorse a political revolution in which government leadership would go not to the politicians but to the actors who even more strikingly looked the part."[23]

While candidates use show-business techniques, it is important that they criticize them. Joe McGinniss noted that Nixon assailed the "damn image experts" and concluded that a candidate "should express distaste for television and suspicion that there is something 'phony' about it. The sophisticated candidate, while analyzing his own on-the-air technique as carefully as a golf pro studies his swing, will state frequently that there is no place for public relations gimmicks or 'those show business guys' in the campaign."[24]

Congressman Ted Weiss from Manhattan told us that he expects the next president to be a fresh face. The media experts want a hardworking, competent person with a decent record but one who doesn't have a strong image on any particular issue. Media consultants can then assess the current vogues in public thinking and encourage the candidate to follow them. The candidate should promise almost everything to everyone. We say *almost* because the candidate has to take into account growing cynicism and be careful to appear to be reasonable. Weiss also indicated that today candidates don't often take real positions on most issues. He believes this will lead to further disappointment and cynicism. He noted that although candidates have more access to the media and there is more exposure than ever before in our history, we don't know any more about our candidates and may know even less. Politicians can use the media to build their suitability as targets (that is, their image) without really revealing anything about their positions on the issues.

We have no need to project the hero if we are in the process of actualizing the hero within, that is, if we are willing and able to fight an inner war. Greed, brutality, the root of evil lie within. To integrate our own inferior qualities necessitates a tremendous struggle. Self-realization requires the utmost heroic efforts.

Although today's American political scene offers few charismatic figures (people who can contain an archetypal projection), we do not think this is because more people are integrating their archetypes. In fact, the disillusionment that occurs a year or so after each election brings with it greater anger and despair. The tension that comes from lacking a target on whom we can project the hero image is increasing. Although Hollywood offers us screen heroes, we seem to need more than this.

Our need for heroes is so great that our lack has the potential to lead to great harm or great good. Our discomfort could turn to the desperation that brought about the rise of Hitler or it could lead in another, new direction. We can stop looking outside ourselves to leaders to solve our problems and hold our projections and start looking within. This process would mean turning away from "spectator politics" and toward "participatory" grass-roots movements. On a psychological level, we would be withdrawing our hero projections from others and developing these qualities ourselves.

9

Conclusions

Although the idea of projection has been alluded to by philosophers, poets, writers, and historians, psychologists have taken a different approach to the problem. In recent years, research psychologists have conducted numerous experiments on the topic, while clinicians put the concept to practical use helping their clients dissolve their projections. Researchers conducting scientific experiments have been attempting to discover by controlling and manipulating variables if projection operates, how it operates, and why it operates. Although there is no longer any doubt that projection occurs, we do not really know how it does so. How can a need or feeling or thought that belongs to you end up looking like it is coming from someone else?

Current Research

Do we simply mistakenly "think" that other people possess traits that they don't? One experiment shows that people actually "look" different due to projection. In his doctoral dissertation, Morton Kissen asked people to look at a group of photographs from a series that ranged from extreme happiness at one end to extreme sadness at the other. Later, when the subjects saw the whole range of photographs and were asked to pick out the ones they had previously seen, they selected ones in accordance with their mood of the moment. This second part of the experiment was called the *recognition task*. People who were happy during the recognition task erroneously selected photographs from the happy end of the scale, and people who were sad erroneously selected photographs from the sadder end.[1] In other words, the emotional state of the person seemed to affect the perception of the physiognomic properties of the photographs. Much more research needs to be done to investigate how actual perceptual and cognitive processes are related to projection.

Not only do psychologists not fully understand how projection operates, but also they are not clear about the function it serves. Within the field, there has been much recent disagreement centering around whether or not projection serves a self-defensive function. Some researchers argue that projection acts as a defense mechanism,[2] while others say that it does not reduce stress and therefore doesn't really defend us against anything.[3]

Most clinicians or psychotherapists would probably agree partially with both points of view. When we project, we *attempt* to reduce stress by expelling feelings or thoughts that are not part of our self-image. However, our attempts to make our lives more satisfying by projection do not work. If we lie and cheat on taxes and see other people as doing so (parallel projection), or deny our desires to cheat and exaggerate these qualities in others (unconscious projection), or deny all our negative asocial qualities and see evil in the world (mythic projection of the shadow), we do not really feel better; we simply exchange threat from within for threat from without. Instead of perceiving our own threatening qualities, the world and other people appear threatening and dangerous. This is why both theoretical viewpoints are valid— projection involves the attempt to defend oneself, but it is ultimately unsuccessful.

As long as we believe that other people are responsible for our emotional lives, there is little we can do.

Dissolving Projections by Assimilating Them

Clinicians or psychotherapists who write about projection seem to be in agreement on how projections can be dissolved. They suggest that we must recognize that what affects us in others comes partly from ourselves. We then need to become conscious of what we project. Different therapists refer to the process as "owning," "becoming conscious," "assimilating," and "identifying with" our projections.

Jungian analysts and Gestalt therapists help their clients work with the projections that are in dreams. Frederick Perls, the founder of Gestalt therapy, developed techniques for working intensively with dreams. In the following reported dream, the Gestalt approach to projection is illustrated.

A man who reports that he feels self-confident, attractive, and bright enters therapy because he is mysteriously beset by anxiety. He reports the following dream: "I am sitting near a brook listening to the sounds of the water, crickets and looking at the embankment on the other side where I see a cigarette butt and a frog. The frog jumps into the water and disappears behind a rock."

Gestalt therapists believe that all the elements of a dream are unowned fragments of the dreamer's personality—projections. The dreamer does not identify with these parts of himself, and he sees them as being outside him. The therapist therefore asks the client to role-play all the elements in the dream—to become the projections. "Be the frog," says the therapist. "Imagine what it is like to really be the frog in your dream." "Okay," says the client, "I am swimming around in the water, but I feel uncomfortable because I have green bumpy skin with black splotches. I swim under some mud so no one can see me." "Aha!" says the Gestalt therapist. The client experiences stage fright. He is very self-conscious. He may be competent and good-looking but he is repressing his self-doubts and his inner concerns. Instead of experiencing these negative thoughts directly, he felt anxiety. By pretending to be the frog—by becoming his projection—the client was able to experience some of these self-doubts and insecurities directly. In time, he is able to integrate these feelings with his confident ones, thereby developing a more realistic and complete self-concept. By perceiving directly the weaknesses in his personality, he can work on changing them. The therapist could also ask the client to identify with the brook, a cricket, and the cigarette butt. Each is seen as a projection of the client, symbols of the alienated parts of himself. As the client assimilates each of the projections, he increases his potential, his energy, his self-image.

It is hard for many people to remember their dreams. Often people think that it is overly self-involved to write them down and try to be each of the elements. This is not really a problem because our projections are as easy to work with in our world of relationships as in our dreams, and there is an even bigger return on dissolving projections in the real world. Not only do you expand your consciousness, but you may also develop real relationships, those free of illusion.

As we grow and become more conscious, our dreams change. In the course of psychotherapy, as clients become more aware of aspects of themselves, their dreams undergo transformation. Therapists who work by asking their patients to assimilate their projections find that the dream images become more and more complex and interesting. The situation is quite similar as we attempt to dissolve our projections in the waking world. There are many layers of projection separating us from the people around us. To get to see your child clearly, for example, is a task requiring the utmost patience, courage, intelligence, creativity, and emotional maturity. In relationships with your child, all three levels of projection are likely to be operating (parallel, unconscious, and mythical).

At the same time that you can discover yourself in your projections onto others, you can make real contact with others. Self-knowledge and the knowledge of others does not come easily or quickly, nor does it come from reading this book. It is relatively easy to see that other people project; it is somewhat harder to see that we ourselves do, and harder yet to take back our projections. Lately psychologists have been recognizing that the process of development does not end with adolescence. In our thirties and in our seventies, there are likely to be many projections that need working out. Thus in asking the reader to examine his projections, magical cures are not being promised, but this is hardly pessimistic. The fact that we can continue to dissolve and become what was formerly projected is a very interesting long-term project.

One could argue that we are better off living in a world of relationships based on projection. Often it is exciting to be surrounded by stars, heroes, dream boys or girls, demons, and perfect parents. But it is a world of confusion and unreality that cannot last. Projections must break down, bringing sorrow, disappointment, and disillusionment. *Disillusionment* is an especially apt term because although it means we feel sadness, it also means we are free of illusions.

Recognizing Projections

People often ask how they can tell if their relationship to someone is based on projection. There are no foolproof answers, although there are a number of clues or cues. The best clues are your own emotions. If you get upset or carried away, if someone really "gets under your skin," projection is often the cause. A man may be quite gorgeous or really special, but when you become obsessed and overwhelmed, it is likely that you are meeting your dream-boy image rather than a man. Similarly, if someone irritates you to the point of driving you crazy, you could be projecting your

shadow. The reactions of other people can also be helpful in identifying our projections. If a friend says, "I don't know what you
see in her," maybe you are not seeing clearly after all. If everyone
at the office gets along with the new vice-president but you find
him impossible, you may be seeing unowned aspects of yourself in
him.

This book has been organized in terms of the situations in which
people project. It may be useful to examine these situations again
for clues that might alert you to the possibility that projection is
operating. The following examples are meant as thumbnail
sketches to assist the reader in recognizing projections. Before one
can possibly dissolve projections, they must first be recognized.

Parents and Children

Do you overestimate the similarities between yourself and your
child? Are you able to see *differences* between you? What are
the differences? If you cannot clearly articulate the differences,
you may be using parallel projection.

Can you acknowledge that there is conflict between yourself
and your spouse? If everything in the family seems wonderful
except for one troublesome child, he is probably being scapegoated. He is likely to be receiving unconscious projections
from the whole family.

Can you see weaknesses in your child? If you are overwhelmed
and speechless by his beauty and brilliance and cannot speak
about anything else other than your child's miraculous accomplishments, you may be projecting the mythic magical child.

It is possible to project many qualities onto our parents. We
can scapegoat them or exaggerate their similarity to us, but it is
most likely that we continue either to project the mythical perfect
parent or to experience disappointment because they cannot contain this projection. If you idealize a parent or cannot forgive one,
the projection has not been dissolved.

Couples

When a couple relationship is formed, one of the first projections to break down is parallel. If you live with a person, it is
almost impossible not to recognize differences after a short time.
If you meet someone and believe that you are of one soul and
one mind, you are using parallel projection.

During periods of stress, do you find yourself getting angry with your partner? When you are under pressure, do you look to your partner to anticipate your needs or your moods? It is often under these circumstances that we project parental images onto our mates, expecting them to take care of us and feeling angry or disappointed when they refuse to contain this projection. Do you fight often over money? Perfect parents provide lots of material goods, give us perfect presents and generous allowances, and don't expect their children to cooperate or sacrifice. When we fight over money, often it is because we are attempting to force our mates to contain the projection of the perfect parent as they struggle to escape its pressure.

When we can find no specific reasons for why we feel "head over heels in love" with someone, projection of the anima/animus is often operating. If our world feels magical, if our lover seems too good to be true—he probably is. The feeling of unreality is quite accurate.

On the Job

Do you feel a spirit of comradeship with your co-workers? Do you feel that your relationships with your peers at work are the most satisfying aspect of your job? Do you think that they would support you if you were in trouble, just as you would support them? This is a sign of parallel projection.

Does your boss always make you uncomfortable? Do you see him consistently as extremely impressive and as knowing what is best for you, your co-workers, the company? Do you see him as especially "together," unflappable? Are you convinced his personal life is as successful as his professional one and that it probably would be helpful for you to discuss your personal problems with him? On the other hand, are you usually angry or dissatisfied with the boss? These reactions are triggered by the projection of parental images.

Is there someone at work who really annoys you? Has there always been someone at work you find irritating? Do you complain often about particular people whom you see as manipulative, shirking, irresponsible, incompetent? If such a person leaves or is fired, does another extremely annoying person emerge to make your life miserable? These are all indications that the shadow is being projected.

Stars and Fans

How do you feel about your favorite entertainer of the same sex? Do you feel you know what kind of person he or she really is? Do you admire the person as much or more than his or her acting, singing, or dancing ability? Do you especially like this person because in real life, he seems to be following his own path, seems to take risks, struggles against evil, tries to be helpful? Would it disappoint you to see your favorite entertainer of the same sex play the part of someone lazy or sloppy or play a villain? Do you think you would be disappointed to read that he was not generous, not kind to his family, and held political views opposite to yours? If so, you are projecting the mythic image of hero onto this entertainer.

How do you feel about your favorite entertainer of the opposite sex? Would you go out with him or her? If you are a woman, are you fascinated by his power, his deeds, his words, or his wisdom? If you are a man, do her beauty, sexuality, nurturing qualities, and wisdom mesmerize you? These qualities say nothing about acting talent or ability; instead, they describe the archetypes of the anima/animus. When we are fascinated with an entertainer and curious about whom they are going out with, perhaps even feeling jealous of their lovers, we are likely to be projecting our own mythic images.

Politics and the News

Although you are horrified by stories of murder, exploitation, war, and battle, do you follow each and every gruesome story to the end? Are you angered and fascinated by stories of corrupt politicians, welfare cheats, crooked businessmen? Are there ethnic groups, countries, politicians you love to hate? Without such enemies, does your life feel less meaningful, purposeful, less full? These are likely to be signs of projecting the shadow.

Can you articulate why you admire the public figures and politicians you do? Do you have a clear undestanding of their positions on the issues? If not, are you mostly impressed by their style, their charisma? Are you mostly enthusiastic about new public figures—ones who show promise and potential? These dynamics indicate the projection of the hero.

We say that the beginning of every presidential administration is a "honeymoon period." What we are acknowledging with this phrase is that our feelings about political figures are based on projections of ideal images and in this initial period they are intact. Are you consistently hopeful, full of expectations and enthusiasm at the beginning of an administration and disappointed shortly thereafter? Disappointment sets in when the projection comes out of phase with the real person; we see someone quite different from our projection of the hero image and we don't like what we see.

Patterns of Projection

One of the best guides for finding your projections is to examine your own patterns in relationships. Do you often become infatuated with someone, fall head over heels in love, and then become disappointed? Do you feel persecuted at work no matter whom you are working with? If we step back from our lives for a moment, patterns are often revealed that show that we are projecting the same images upon a number of different targets.

"I have the worst luck when it comes to men. I always seem to get hooked up with people who have no interest in a commitment, in a real relationship. Things start out all right, but quickly I become the one who calls them or waits by the phone. I'm the one who gets stood up. I always end up making concessions, taking care of everything, being responsible for everything, understanding when he can't meet me. And I'm the one who ends up hurt. Even though I often think I should break it off, somehow I never get around to doing it first—so I'm the one who's left. I hope my luck changes soon. My life is not easy. I'm alone with a three-year-old kid who needs a lot of discipline."

Thelma is a twenty-five-year-old woman who feels completely out of control and powerless in her relationships with men. She puts a great deal of faith in luck—but *luck* really has little to do with it. She is really at no one's mercy but her own. Thelma feels that she can't do anything about the quality and outcome of her relationships because "I don't have the power to change anyone else." This is true. However, like many of us, she gives other people too much credit for her life. She could change her "luck" by looking at the part she plays in her problems, that is, by acquainting herself with her own unconscious projections.

Thelma had a difficult childhood, with a father who often seemed on the verge of abandoning the family. At an early age, she set out to please him and thus keep him at home. In order to do this, she had to become rather manipulative. As an adult, Thelma feels fooled, betrayed, and manipulated in her relationships with men. When she first starts seeing a man, he seems caring, strong, honest, and committed. However, after a while, she begins to feel betrayed and taken advantage of. She's always amazed at how badly they fooled her. This pattern can be understood in terms of projection. Thelma is unconscious of her own need to manipulate and control others, as she sought to manipulate and control her childhood situation. This unacceptable characteristic—this aspect of her shadow—remains unconscious and is projected on those around her. She sees others as being deceitful and manipulative. Because she has not made a successful separation from her parents, this projection onto men guarantees that she will remain loyal to her father by unconsciously sabotaging her relationships with men.

When people understand how projection works in one aspect of their lives, they usually begin to see it operating in other areas. Not only do we project in a variety of situations; different situations can trigger similar projections. That is, there is a pattern that crosses over into different areas of our lives. Thelma is a good case in point. She not only feels exploited by men, she also finds herself at odds with her boss and co-workers because she feels that they take advantage of her at work. She struggles with her child because she feels he is undisciplined. All these instances show a pattern—they signal the projection of socially unacceptable feelings, the need to dominate and control. Instead of acknowledging those qualities, Thelma projects them. It is a useful exercise to try to identify what it is about the person we might be having a problem with or that we dislike. A simple list is enough. Compare the list about your spouse to the one about your boss or your least favorite politician.

The idea that we are confusing our own feelings with the feelings of others—that we are mistaken about the intent of their actions, that even their physical appearance is not clear to us, that our psychological needs and our emotions act as a filter through which we perceive (or misperceive) the world—is scary. A number of different people have said, "If what you say is true and I'm just projecting, then I don't know what I'm doing. I might as well give up because I don't know what's going on. Everything I thought I knew about the people around me is wrong."

When people say things like this, they feel they are *out of control.* They no longer can believe their own senses. But being able to understand and identify your projections really gives you greater control over your life and your relationships. Projection involves energy and control, which, when you project, you believe other people have over you. By considering that *we* create our problems, we can take the responsibility to find solutions. This is true both on an individual level as well as on a much wider one. Our inability to take responsibility for ourselves and our tendency to project the shadow seem to be as prevalent today as they were in 1937, when Jung wrote the following passage:

> Look at the incredible savagery going on in our so-called civilized world: it all comes from human beings.... Look at the devilish engines of destruction! They are invented by completely innocuous gentlemen, reasonable respectable citizens who are everything we could wish. And when the whole thing blows up, and an indescribable hell of destruction is let loose, nobody seems to be responsible. It simply happens, and yet it is all man-made. But since everybody is blindly convinced that he is nothing more than his own extremely unassuming and insignificant and conscious self, which performs its duties decently and earns a moderate living, nobody is aware that this whole rationalistically organized conglomeration we call a state or a nation is driven on by a seemingly impersonal invisible but terrifying power which nobody and nothing can check. This ghastly power is mostly explained as fear of the neighboring nation, which is supposed to be possessed by a malevolent fiend. Since nobody is capable of recognizing just where and how much he himself is possessed and unconscious, he simply projects his own condition upon his neighbor, and thus it becomes a sacred duty to have the biggest guns and the most poisonous gas. The worst of it is that he is quite right. All one's neighbors are in the grip of some uncontrolled and uncontrollable fear, just like oneself.[4]

American psychology has consistently focused on the way the environment affects the individual. We are as we are (most psychologists say) because of reinforcement, punishments, social models, economics, social circumstances, family structure, communication patterns in the family, and so on. While this is true, we must also consider that we construct our environments—the people around us—with our perceptions and cognitions. By removing our projections, we can see the world more accurately.

Notes

Notes for Chapter 1

1. For recent experimental reviews see James Halpern, "Projection: A Test of the Psychoanalytic Hypothesis," *Journal of Abnormal Psychology* 86 (1977): 536–42; G.G. Sherwood, "Classical and Attribution Projection," *Journal of Abnormal Psychology* 88 (1979): 635–40; and G.G. Sherwood, "Self-serving Biases in Person Perception: A Reexamination of Projection as a Mechanism of Defense," *Psychological Bulletin* 90 (1981): 445–59.

2. C.G. Jung, "General Aspects of Dream Psychology," in *The Collected Works of C.G. Jung*, 2nd ed., 15 vols. (New Jersey: Princeton University Press, 1954–79), vol. 8, p. 264.

3. Lester Luborsky et al., "Factors Influencing the Outcome of Psychotherapy: A Review of Quantitative Research," *Psychological Bulletin* 75 (1971): 145–85.

4. S.R. Weisman, "Epilogue: For America a Painful Reawakening," *The New York Times Magazine* (special issue: *America in Captivity*), May 17, 1981, p. 117.

Notes for Chapter 2

1. Sigmund Freud, "Extracts from the Fliess Papers," in *The Complete Psychological Works of Sigmund Freud*, 24 vols. (1895; reprint ed., London: Hogarth Press, 1953–74), vol. 1, p. 207.

2. B.I. Murstein, and R.S. Pryor, "The Concept of Projection: A Review," *Psychological Bulletin* 56 (1959): 370.

3. H.A. Murray, Foreword in H.H. Anderson and G.L. Anderson, eds., *An Introduction to Projective Techniques* (Englewood Cliffs, N.J.: Prentice-Hall, 1951), p. 13.

4. Beatrice Wright, "Altruism in Children and the Perceived Conduct of Others," *Journal of Abnormal and Social Psychology* 37 (1942): 218–33.

5. Elizabeth Mintz, "An Example of Assimilative Projection," *Journal of Abnormal and Social Psychology* 52 (1956): 279–80.

6. H.J. Goldings, "On the Avowal and Projection of Happiness," *Journal of Personality* 23 (1954): 30–47.

7. I.E. Bender, and A. Hastorf, "The Perception of Persons: Forecasting

Another Person's Responses on Three Personality Scales," *Journal of Abnormal and Social Psychology* 45 (1950): 556–61.

8. Karen Horney, *New Ways in Psychoanalysis* (New York: Norton, 1939) p. 26.

9. James Halpern and Anne Myers, "Effects of Type of Target, Cognitive Ability and Age on Projection," *Perceptual and Motor Skills*, 46 (1978): 727–30; and Anne Myers and James Halpern, "Attributive and Contrast Projection: A Cognitive Approach," *The Journal of Psychology* (1977): 43–48.

10. Dana Bramel, "A Dissonance Theory Approach to Defensive Projection," *Journal of Abnormal and Social Psychology* 64 (1962): 121–29.

11. Freud, "Extracts from the Fliess Papers," in *The Complete Psychological Works*, vol. 1, pp. 173–280.

12. Freud, "The Unconscious," in *The Complete Psychological Works*, vol. 14, pp. 159–215.

13. Freud, "Some Neurotic Mechanisms in Jealousy, Paranoia, and Homosexuality," in *The Complete Psychological Works*, vol. 18, pp. 223–32.

14. Ibid., p. 226.

15. Freud, "Wild Psychoanalysis," in *The Complete Psychological Works*, vol. 11, pp. 219–27.

16. Freud, "Remembering, Repeating and Working Through," in *The Complete Psychological Works*, vol. 12, pp. 145–56.

17. Freud, "The Dynamics of Transference," in *The Complete Psychological Works*, vol. 12, p. 100.

18. Freud, "Psychoanalytic Notes upon an Autobiographical Account of a Case of Paranoia," in *The Complete Psychological Works*, vol. 12, p. 71.

19. James Halpern, "Projection: A Test of the Psychoanalytic Hypothesis," *Journal of Abnormal Psychology* 86 (1977): 536–42.

20. C.G. Jung, *Analytical Psychology: Its Theory and Practice* (New York: Random House, Vintage Books, 1968), p. 163.

21. Ibid., pp. 87–105.

22. C.G. Jung, *Memories, Dreams, Reflections.* (New York: Random House, Vintage Books, 1961), p. 392.

23. C.G. Jung, "Civilization in Transition," in *The Collected Works of C.G. Jung,* 2nd ed., 15 vols. (New Jersey: Princeton University Press, 1954–79), vol. 10, p. 26.

24. Jung, "The Structure and Dynamics of the Psyche," in *The Collected Works*, vol. 8, p. 273.

25. Jung, "Aion: Researches into the Phenomenology of the Self," in *The Collected Works*, vol. 9, part 2, p. 9.

26. Jung, *Analytical Psychology: Its Theory and Practice* (New York: Random House, Vintage Books, 1968), p. 160.

Notes for Chapter 3

1. Wayne Sage, "Violence in the Children's Room," *Human Behavior* 4 (1975): 7:40–47.

2. Blair Justice and Rita Justice, *The Abusing Family* (New York: Human Sciences Press, 1976).

3. E.A. Carter and M. McGoldrick, eds., *The Family Life Cycle: A Framework for Family Therapy* (New York: Gardner Press, 1980).

4. C.G. Jung, "The Psychology of the Child Archetype," in *The Collected Works of C. G. Jung*, 2nd ed., 15 vols. (New Jersey: Princeton University Press, 1954–79), vol. 9, part 1, pp. 151–81.

5. Jay Haley, *Problem Solving Therapy: New Strategies for Effective Family Therapy* (New York: Harper Colophon, 1978).

6. ———, *Leaving Home: The Therapy of Disturbed Young People* (New York: McGraw-Hill, 1980).

7. R.D. Laing, *The Politics of the Family and Other Essays* (New York: Random House, Vintage Books, 1972), p. 67.

8. Theodor Adorno et al. *The Authoritarian Personality* (New York: Harper, 1950).

Notes for Chapter 4

1. See E.M. Hetherington, "Effects of Father Absence on Personality Development in Adolescent Daughters," *Developmental Psychology* 7 (1972): 313–26; J.B. Kelly and J.S. Wallerstein, "The Effects of Parental Divorce: Experiences of the Child in Early Latency," *American Journal of Orthopsychiatry* 46 (1976): 20–32; J.F. McDermott, "Divorce and Its Psychiatric Sequelae in Children, "*Archives of General Psychiatry* 23 (1970): 421–27; and J.S. Wallerstein and J.B. Kelly, "The Effects of Parental Divorce: Experiences of the Preschool Child," *Journal of the American Academy of Child Psychiatry* 14 (1975): 600–16.

2. B.L. Bloom, S.J. Asher, and S.W. White, "Marital Disruption as a Stressor: A Review and Analysis," *Psychological Bulletin* 85 (1978): 867–94.

3. Donn Byrne, "Attitudes and Attraction," in *Advances in Experimental Social Psychology*, vol. 4, ed. L. Berkowitz (New York: Academic Press, 1969).

4. James Halpern and Mark A. Sherman, *Afterplay: A Key to Intimacy* (New York: Stein and Day, 1979).

5. Carl Rogers, *On Becoming a Person* (Boston: Houghton Mifflin, 1961).

6. W.H. Masters and V.E. Johnson, *Human Sexual Inadequacy* (Boston: Little Brown, 1970).

7. Suzanne K. Steinmetz and Murray A. Straus, "The Family as Cradle of Violence," *Society* 10 (1973): 6:50–56.

Notes for Chapter 5

1. Karen Dion and Ellen Berscheid, "Physical Attractiveness and Sociometric Choice in Nursery School Children," cited by Elliot Aronson in *The Social Animal*, 3rd ed. (San Francisco: W.H. Freeman, 1980).

2. Karen Dion, "Physical Attractiveness and Evaluations of Children's Transgressions," *Journal of Personality and Social Psychology* 24 (1972): 207–13.

3. Harold Sigall and Elliot Aronson, "Liking for an Evaluator as a Function of Her Physical Attractiveness and Nature of the Evaluations," *Journal of Experimental Social Psychology* 5 (1969): 93–100.

4. Gregory Bateson et al., "Toward a Theory of Schizophrenia," *Behavioral Science* 1 (1956): 251–64.

5. US Bureau of the Census, *Current population reports. Number, Timing, and Duration of Marriages and Divorces in the United States: June, 1975* (series no. 297, p. 20) (Washington, D.C.: US Government Printing Office, 1976).

Notes for Chapter 6

1. F.J. Roethlisberger, *Man in Organization: Essays of F. J. Roethlisberger* (Washington, D.C.: Howard University Press, 1968) pp. 104–5.

2. Ibid., pp. 98–99.

3. Joseph Heller, *Something Happened* (New York: Knopf, 1974), p. 13.

4. Elliot Aronson, *The Social Animal*, 3rd. ed. (San Francisco: W.H. Freeman, 1980), pp. 180–82.

5. Carl Hovland and Robert Sears, "Minor Studies of Aggression: Correlations of Lynchings with Economic Indices," *Journal of Psychology* 9 (1940): 301–10.

6. Douglas Bauer, "Why Big Business Is Firing the Boss," *The New York Times Magazine*, March 8, 1981, 22–91.

7. Ibid.

Notes for Chapter 7

1. *The New York Daily News*, 23 June 1981, 1.

2. *The New York Times*, 2 April 1981, 24.

3. *People*, 20 April 1981, 38.

4. C.G. Jung, *Memories, Dreams, Reflections* (New York: Random House, Vintage Books, 1961), p. 392.

5. Philip Norman, *Shout* (New York: Simon & Schuster, 1981), p. 220.

6. Jung, *Memories, Dreams, Reflections*, p. 391.

7. Emma Jung, *Animus and Anima* (New York: The Analytical Psychology Club of New York, 1957), p. 10.

8. C.G. Jung, "The Development of Personality," in *The Collected Works of C. G. Jung*, 2nd ed., 15 vols. (New Jersey: Princeton University Press, 1954–79), vol. 17, p. 198.

9. E. Jung, *Animus and Anima*, p. 46.

10. Elliot Aronson, *The Social Animal*, 3rd ed. (San Francisco: W.H. Freeman, 1980), 93.

11. Barney Cohen, Burt Reynolds: Going Beyond Macho," *The New York Times Magazine*, 29 March 1981, 56.

12. Norman Zierold, *Garbo* (New York: Stein & Day, 1969) pp. 55, 14.

Notes for Chapter 8

1. Tony Schwartz, "When News Goes Show Biz," *The New York Times*, 9 August 1981, 23.

2. Mark R. Levy, quoted in *Time*, 1 October 1979, p. 83.

3. Konrad Lorenz, *On Aggression* (New York: Harcourt Brace and World, 1966).

4. Sigmund Freud, *Civilization and Its Discontents* (1930; reprint ed., New York: W.W. Norton, 1962), p. 58.

5. C.G. Jung, "Psychology and Religion," in *The Collected Works of C.G. Jung*, 2nd ed., 15 vols. (New Jersey: Princeton University Press, 1954–79), vol. 11, p. 76.

6. Freud, p. 61.

7. Theodor Adorno et al., *The Authoritarian Personality* (New York: Harper, 1950).

8. John Darnton, "Anti-Semitism without Jews? A Polish riddle," *The New York Times*, 14 March 1981.

9. Hermann Rauschning, *Hitler Speaks* (London: Thornton Butterworth, 1939), p. 233.

10. Ibid.

11. Aristotle, *The Politics of Aristotle*, ed. and trans. Ernest Becker (London: Oxford University Press, 1977), p. 226.

12. Adolf Hitler, *My New Order* (speeches ed. by Raoul de Roussy de Sales) (New York: Reynal and Hitchcock, 1941), p. 661.

13. Ibid., p. 685.

14. Ibid., p. 687.

15. S.R. Weisman, "Epilogue: For America a Painful Reawakening," *The New York Times Magazine* (Special issue: *America in Captivity*) May 17, 1981, p. 117.

16. Joseph Campbell, *The Hero with a Thousand Faces*, 2nd ed. (New Jersey: Princeton University Press, 1968).

17. Dan Nimmo and J.E. Combs, *Subliminal Politics* (New Jersey: Prentice-Hall, 1980).

18. Nicholas Cords and Patrick Gerster, *Myth in American History* (New York: Glencoe Press, 1977).

19. E. Aronson, B. Willerman, and J. Floyd, "The Effect of a Pratfall on Increasing Interpersonal Attractiveness," *Psychonomic Science* 4 (1966): 227–28.

20. Joseph McGinniss, *The Selling of the President* (New York: Trident Press, 1969), p. 155.

21. Jeff Greenfield, *Playing to Win* (New York: Simon and Schuster, 1980).

22. *The New Yorker,* 30 June 1980, 67.
23. Ibid., 69.
24. McGinniss, p. 53.

Notes for Chapter 9

1. Morton Kissen, "A Demonstration of Certain Effects of Emotional States upon Perception," unpublished doctoral dissertation, Graduate Faculty, New School for Social Research, 1968.

2. G.G. Sherwood, "Self-serving Biases in Person Perception: A Reexamination of Projection as a Mechanism of Defense," *Psychological Bulletin,* 90 (1981): 445–59.

3. D.S. Holmes, "Existence of Classical Projection and the Stress-reducing Function of Attributive Projection: A Reply to Sherwood," *Psychological Bulletin* 90 (1981): 460–66.

4. C.G. Jung, "Psychology and Religion," in *The Collected Works of C.G. Jung,* 2nd. ed., vol. 11 (New Jersey: Princeton University Press, 1969), p. 48.